LORDS
OF LIGHT

The Path of Initiation in the
Western Mysteries

W. E. Butler

LORDS OF LIGHT

The Path of Initiation in the Western Mysteries

THE TEACHINGS OF
THE IBIS FRATERNITY

W . E . BUTLER

Edited by M. A. Geikie

Destiny Books
Rochester, Vermont

Destiny Books
One Park Street
Rochester, Vermont 05767

LIBRARY OF CONGRESS CATALOGING-IN-PUBLICATION DATA

Butler, W. E. (Walter Ernest), 1898–
    Lords of light : the path of initiation in the western mysteries : the
teachings of the ibis fraternity / W. E. Butler : edited by M. A. Geikie.
        p. cm.
    Includes bibliographical references and index.
    ISBN 0-89281-308-3
    1. Occultism. 2. Butler, W. E. (Walter Ernest), 1898–
Interviews. 3. Occultists—Interviews. I. Geikie. M. A.
II. Title
BF1408.2.B88A5   1990
135—dc20   90–23738
                                                                CIP

Printed and bound in the United States

10   9   8   7   6   5   4   3   2

Production by the Park Street Press Group

Destiny Books is a division of Inner Traditions International, Ltd.

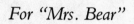

For "Mrs. Bear"

CONTENTS

Publisher's Note

Lords of Light is the transcript of a course of training in the Western Mystery Tradition given by the late Reverend W. E. Butler from March 31 to April 2, 1978, at the Ibis Fraternity Mystery School, Old Domons House, Bratton-Clovelly, Devon, England.

It was Mr. Butler's wish that should these lectures come to be published, they should first be edited and revised by M. A. Geikie, Warden of Ibis Fraternity. Inquiries regarding the Ibis Fraternity should be addressed to:

Mrs. Estella Machin
Director of Studies
5 Trecarne Close, Polgooth
St. Austell, Cornwall
PL25 7BS, England

W. E. BUTLER:
A REMEMBRANCE

These teaching lectures were the last public work that Ernest (W. E.) Butler was to give. Four months later he was on his way to those pearly gates of which he spoke in his introductory lecture. He was far from feeling well at the time, and it was against his doctor's express orders that he travelled from Southampton to Devon; but as he himself put it, he was obeying a higher authority.

So he came, with his "tin leg" (his terminology) accompanied by Mrs. Butler, his beloved and caring "Mrs. Bear." A member of Ibis Fraternity brought them by car to ensure he could at least travel in comparative comfort. Although his good leg was giving him pain throughout, he never allowed his personal discomfort to surface during teaching sessions. There was no doubt that he had the mind-over-matter technique buttoned up to the nth degree.

His was what one might describe as a merry face, rosy cheeks and twinkling eyes, reminiscent of a mischievous elf. This was the Mr. Butler the students knew and respected. Few of them were aware how ill he really was. Not until the lecture door had closed behind him did he give any indication of the pain that tormented him. Even then he treated it as a lesser soul might complain of a headache.

Making for his own special chair, he would plump himself down and say, "What about a cup of tea for the old man then? This damned foot's giving me hell." Four months later that same hell was to lead to a second amputation and to his ultimate passing on.

He had a close, uncanny relationship with animals. At that time we had two standard poodles and two Burmese cats, with frequent spurts of rivalry between them. All four claimed Ernest as their own special friend. Muffin, the younger Burmese, who was especially possessive, determined it was his privilege to sit on Ernest's lap, and the two of them would doze together in perfect harmony with the fireguard arranged round Ernest's foot to prevent animals and humans alike from barging into it.

Ibis Fraternity was the child of his old age. He had recently retired from the Servants of the Light Association, handing over the directorship to Dolores Ashcroft-Nowicki. This left a gap, and like Mother Nature herself, Ernest abhored a vacuum, so Ibis Fraternity was born. Its purpose, while keeping a low profile, was to help and teach other seekers on the Path of the Mysteries.

He served the Mysteries gladly and with a rare dedication for over sixty years. He frequently affirmed that without the love and backing of Gladys, his wife, he would have been hard put to carry on.

To the impatient or the despondent he would quote this verse:

> *Let no man think that sudden in a minute*
> *All is accomplished and the work is done;*
> *Though with thy earliest dawn thou shouldst*
>   *begin it*
> *Scarce were it ended in thy setting sun.*[1]

M. A. Geikie
Warden Ibis Fraternity

INTRODUCTION

I thought that in tonight's talk, which is really an informal one, I would try to discuss with you some of the ideas I have concerning the occult order of things. I say, discuss with you, as I hope that when I've finished there will be questions you will wish to ask. And I don't mind questions, I love 'em! "Question and Answer" has always been the traditional method of occult education, the old way of doing things, and the way I have had to follow for over sixty years. "Question and Answer"—so that we have a true drawing-out from your minds of some of your ideas in response to my particular propositions; in this way we have the clash of ideas from which truth spills out. Then we begin to see each other's points of view and another angle to that which we already have. Sometimes we fall into the teacher-pupil attitude, and I don't want you to regard me as a teacher. I am not going to regard you as pupils, but as fellow travellers on the path. I am going to approach you as people who also have their own points of view and methods of approach. All I can give you is a stimulus to your own thinking. If I simply opened my mouth and poured my thinking into you like syrup, you might get a little intellectual surface knowledge; but it would flow in and flow out again. It might possibly cause a little trouble on the way if it upset some of your convictions, but otherwise it wouldn't produce anything.

What I would like to do is to sow a few seeds which will possibly bear fruit, but fruit which belongs to you. There's no monopoly of knowledge; not one of us can say we are the people who are qualified to say whether a thing is or is not. We are all of us ignorant in varying degrees, some more than others. No one is perfect; no one is infallible. We are all liable to make mistakes; none of us has the right to assume we are the divinely appointed teacher of humanity. We are all together, you and I, as students and followers of the way. Incidentally, that title was one of the greatest of the early Christian Church. Before they were ever called Christians in Antioch, they were known as the "Followers of the Way." Each one of us is a follower of the way. You and I have been bitten by the same bug. Whereas the average person doesn't worry about understanding, we want to know; we want to try to understand. And it is promised that if we truly want to know, then the teacher will come; and we shall have the power to know. The very fact of wanting to know presupposes there is someone who can give us the answers.

We're looking for a teacher; we're looking for a new aspect of philosophy, something or someone who will explain to us something about life itself. Knowledge cannot be in a vacuum; it must always be related to other things. You can have someone that is all knowledge, so full that it shakes out of their ears every time they move; and yet they may not have enough sense to come in out of the rain. Go to Oxford or Cambridge and see some of the dons around there. They're chock-full of knowledge; you couldn't fault them. But when it comes to understanding the world and its problems, any one of them can be as big a fool as you or I. They may have a lot of knowledge, but wisdom has passed them by. So we ask not only for knowledge but for wisdom too. And the answer is, "Yes, you can have that knowledge; you can attain that wisdom." But first of all, why do you want it? Do you want it simply in order that you may be about three inches above the average height? Do you want it to add a cubit or so to your mental stature so that you can go around performing funny little tricks to the awe and amazement of your fellow men? A lot of people do. This is why they hunt out this teacher and that teacher, this guru and that guru, trying to find a way in which they can gain this self-aggrandizement. That's really the false ego trying to get what it thinks it needs. But that leads nowhere. Those who follow that line gain; they gain what they want, only to find they cannot use it. They make mistakes and it turns round and rends them; they're back where they started, only worse off, because now they're faced with a long, long slope to reclimb.

So first: what is our motive? If I want knowledge, why do I want it? And of course you can be terribly self-misleading about this question. Well, I want knowledge so that I can understand more of the universe, why things happen and how they happen. I want this knowledge because it will help me to understand and know something about God. I want all kinds of things. I want to advance myself so that I can call myself a dedicated disciple, an initiate, an adept. Well, you can do all those things, but they are not the real reasons. There is only one reason. . . .

I remember, a good many years ago now, coming blindfolded to the door of the lodge into which I was to be initiated. I knocked at the door, and a voice from within called out, "Who stands at the door of the lodge?" Whereupon I answered, "One who seeks admittance to your lodge." The voice within asked, "Why do you seek admission to our lodge to learn of our teachers?" And I gave the answer, the only acceptable answer, "I desire to know in order to serve." It was of course a symbolic answer, the formal entrée into the lodge, but the reality was there all the same. And that is the key to all occult teaching: If you "desire to know in order to serve," then sooner or later you will obtain that knowledge. If you desire to know for any lesser purpose, you will not receive the fullness of that knowledge.

Service—to love your neighbor as yourself and, equally, to love yourself as your neighbor—don't forget it cuts both ways. I think it was Solomon who said, "I will not offer that to the Lord which has cost me nothing."[1] We each of us bring ourselves to the sacrificial altar to offer ourselves—the same as in the communion service in the church; we offer ourselves to be "a reasonable, holy, and living sacrifice in spirit, soul, and body." And what have we offered? Not something which is really perfect, not something that is really good, but something which we haven't worried about; we haven't even brushed its hair before we took it up for the sacrifice. There are many things we could do to ourselves before we knock at that door. But we don't do them. We think we have the right to go barging through the door and say, "Here I am, I want to be taught." Whereupon we're politely conducted outside again and told, "No." Service, true service, is the only key. And that is the reason, service to ourselves, to make of ourselves true sacrifices, to give something worthwhile, to make of ourselves a jewel. And that means occult training. And occult training doesn't mean just sitting down and reading books by W. E. Butler or Dion Fortune or Colin Wilson or anybody like that. Books mean nothing in themselves. They're handy compilations of odds and ends, but you can't put reality into a book.

I remember when I first went out on an astral projection and realized I was a living spirit who didn't depend on the body. That's the first realization that comes to you with astral projection. I realized, standing looking down on my body, "That's me, but I'm here too. This is me, the real person; the other's only my body which I've been using." Once you get that realization into your mind, then death ceases to cause any fear at all. Absolutely! That was the vital thing in the old mysteries; when they were properly performed, the initiate lost all fear of death. Those who have passed through that gate lose all fear of death. Mark you, I don't say I'm not afraid of dying, that's another matter. I'm a coward and don't like bodily pain; therefore, I hope that when I do pass through those pearly gates it will be a painless passing. But the actual state of death doesn't worry me two hoots, because I know. I don't just "believe." I know. I don't take it on anybody else's word, but from my own personal experience of sixty-four years in the occult world. I know that I shall still live.

See the difference between knowledge and gnosis, the absolute conviction. You find it very often in the writings of St. Paul where he rightly gets going and says, "I'm absolutely convinced." No argument, no question of this, that, or the other. And so it is with any of us who have passed through that gate. But there's more to it than that: to pass through that gate and come in contact with others, some who are temporarily where you are, some who are permanently removed, brings to you the idea that you are not on your own. In one way you are, of course, inasmuch as each one of us feels his/her own personal identity; you're you and I'm I, and never the twain shall meet. But there are phases of consciousness (again which you can understand, but which you have to experience in order for them to become part of your knowledge, part of your very being), and these experiences convince you in a way that knowledge by itself does not. They convince you that you are linked with every form of life in this universe, that you are part of the living universe.

There is nothing that is alien to you, nothing with which you have not some contact, some part. We talk about man being a spark of the Divine. The Divine by definition is the Eternal, the Infinite. And one thing you cannot do: you cannot carve the Infinite into segments as you would an apple. Any part of the Infinite remains the Infinite. That is what is meant by the theological term the "omnipresence of God." God is everywhere and there is nowhere he is not, and there is no way you can divide the Infinity. Your spirit and my spirit are both sparks from the flame. We are that flame because sparks can never be divided from the flame. So the Eternal Spirit, Who works and energizes in the cosmos of which we are a part, is dwelling, is working, is energizing in you and me also. Now that is one of the things we have to learn in occultism in order to get a due sense of proportion.

When the old initiate of the Greek Mysteries came to the well where the White Tree grew, the guardians stopped him and asked, "Who are you?" (The same thing happened in the Egyptian Mysteries.) When he came to the pillars of the gateway, they stopped him and asked, "Who are you?" And, "Who am I?" The initiate had to answer both questions. In the Greek Mysteries, he would reply to the first question, "I am a child of earth, this ye know. But my race is from the starry heavens." And each of us is a child of earth, with all the passions, with all the dirtiness, all the beastliness of the animal kingdom from which we've come, still in us.

If we acknowledge the shadow in ourselves, as it is within everyone, then we shall have a truer picture of ourselves. Although Jung calls it the "shadow," it is, in fact, part of the "dweller of the threshold" of occult tradition. We are, first of all, children of earth, and we draw from the Earth Mother and from the racial past those things which belong to the earth. But we are also from the starry heavens. Having regard for these two facts, we shall see that our job is to unite the two. Now, how are we going to do that? Religion means to bind back, and, in this case, we're to bind back to God. If there is the Eternal (called "the Ground of the Soul" in Catholic theology) in each one of us, then that is what we're going to be bound back to. So we have no need to look to this teacher and that teacher. As Jesus said, "The Kingdom of God is within you." And within us too is that teacher who is the greatest teacher we shall ever meet, the God within us. We can call him "the Higher Self, the Holy Guardian Angel." We can give him any name we like— "Adonai, the Lord," any name—but it is from that teacher we shall ultimately learn, because he is the only true teacher. Still, teaching is only half the story.

The pupil-teacher relationship, guru and chela, is a mistaken one because in true education, the teacher and the taught are linked together. And, just as the scientist cannot observe a scientific experiment without altering the nature of the experiment by his presence, by his very being, you cannot come into any kind of relationship with inner things without being affected by them and without your own personality entering into it and being torn to pieces.

The path is not a path for those who are wanting something; it is a path for those who are going to be something, who are going to take of themselves and forge from themselves an instrument in the hands of the Divine. We are going to offer ourselves, all of ourselves, everything in us, to the Eternal. And from the Eternal comes the gnosis, the knowledge that is above knowledge. This inner gnosis, which is far above knowledge, is taught us by the teacher-who-dwells-within. But teaching is not just a question of knowing, of learning something; the mind is always trying to do that, always trying to make forms into which we can construct our miniature universe. As you know, we all construct a universe for ourselves; sometimes it is "penny plain," sometimes "tuppence colored." But every one of us constructs our own universe; we wait for someone to come along and kick it; then we react violently or otherwise, according to our natures. But that creative instinct is right. We have to create our own universe, but it has to be built upon the true lines. Just as David received the pattern of the Temple on the Mountain and passed it on to Solomon, his son, who actually built the temple, we have to go into the mountain of exalted consciousness—we have to reach up within to gain the plan, the blueprint by which we can construct our universe here in the world.

Well, that's the job of treading the path, not a question of becoming an adept overnight. Not a question of trying to become someone big, but a question of taking part in the greatest work in the whole universe. We're going to be universe builders in company with God. We are going to be tools, instruments in the hands of the Eternal as His will prevails in the universes which He has formed and in which He lives, moves, and has His being and which He is bringing back to perfection from their fallen state. And you and I have the privilege of being coworkers with Him and with the whole of creation which is part of His work. That is what occultism is to me. That is what I have been taught over the years.

There are no kudos, no particular merit at all, just a lot of hard work. And I would not be honest with you if I didn't say to you: unless you really feel drawn towards the occult world, unless you really feel you want to change your lesser universe into something more in line with the divine world, unless you are prepared to take on mental and spiritual work of a very exhausting nature—then leave occultism alone.

The path of evolution is proceeding; mankind is evolving, albeit very slowly. Sometimes you think it's going backwards, but no; it is evolving. You might liken it to a great crowd of people marching along the road, a spiral road going round and round a hill (the hill is Abiegnus, the Rosicrucian Mount),[2] and humanity's treading that particular road like a flock of sheep, kicking up a lot of dust, going very slowly, stopping now and then, scrapping and biting each other, all getting panicky, running here and there, and just moving, sometimes hardly that.

Now there are those among you who have done that in the past; indeed we all have. But this time you're determined; you're not going to lag behind; you're going to forge ahead; you've pledged yourself: I will now take destiny into my own hands; I desire to know in order to serve, both God and man, not only for this life, but for future lives too. Then you take the path that goes straight up the mountain, the path that bypasses all those slow spirals. Straight up the mountain! But in so doing, you skin your feet; you skin your hands; you get sunburned and blinded—all kinds of things happen to you. You get discouraged and dispirited; then you say, "O Lord, why ever did I try to do anything like this? Here I am trying to be of service and what happens? Destiny lobs large bricks at me. What have I done to deserve it?"

Well, you've done the same thing to deserve it that I did as a machine gunner in the First World War. I took my little gun, pointed it to the right spot and shot at the Germans. Whereupon the other side, quiet until now, suddenly turned the artillery in my direction and there were shells dropping all over the place, trying to blast me out. As soon as you start to be useful in the army, the opposite side begins to get nasty. It's just the same on the occult path. As long as you're sitting in your little trench doing nothing, the other side is perfectly happy. But the moment you try to make yourself into an efficient instrument, the legions prowl around after your blood because they know that if you succeed, you're one more added to the army of light. So don't run away with the idea it's all milk and honey and roses all the way in the occult world. As soon as you start to study occultism, you'll come up against it. You'll find those who are willing to show you a little bit of interesting phenomena, pass on a little bit of interesting philosophy; and on that they will proceed to rook you of your goods, of your honor, of your decency—of your existence, almost. They'll try to dominate and interfere with your life. They come along like flies in summertime because you are now becoming dangerous to the forces of darkness.

Now all this sounds like scaremongering, but it isn't. You might just as well know where the enemy is as be caught unawares one dark night. If you know that these misfortunes which come upon you are the consequences of what you've been doing, you can say to yourself, "Well here they are! Now, can I apply the knowledge I've gained to combat these unfortunate happenings?" If you can say that, then you've won a battle. Don't forget. It's not the easy things of life that give you true occult and spiritual growth. It's the hard things, the obstacles to your passage. Something always tries to prevent you, and you have to fight to keep on going. The setbacks can help you immeasurably if you take them in the right spirit.

The very fact that they disturb and upset you is all to the good because you are like a caterpillar who's changing into a chrysalis. While it's changing into a chrysalis, it's neither a caterpillar nor a chrysalis; it's in a devil of a mess. It must be very painful for a caterpillar. (I haven't been one lately; still, I imagine, it must be a painful process.)

So finally you come into the chrysalis stage. All the old things are behind you; all the old motivations have gone. You don't love because of a pretty face; you don't like because something has an attractive cover; but you love and you like and you work because of a principle, because you now try to do the will of your Father Who is in heaven and Who dwells within you. There comes a time when all the desire for ordinary things has passed—but leaving vital centers still existing within you. You pass through the dark night of the soul, which is a reality (not the thing that people talk about so much). I've heard some people yapping about the dark night of the soul in a way that makes me weep. What they're talking about isn't the dark night of the soul; it's a bit of a tummy ache, that's all. The reality is terrible; it's something that tests you. It's like the potter who used to bang on the pots with an iron rod; if one broke, well, that was it.

We're tested all the way along the line; and if circumstances test us, they also bring out the best in us. And so to return to our chrysalis: there are left in him only those vital centers which are going to produce from a new blueprint not a caterpillar, but a butterfly. If you've ever had the curiosity to examine a chrysalis from the inside, you'd find an amorphous fluid and just one or two spots that seem more solid than others. That is what will be the butterfly. The DNA patterns in the cells of the body begin to build up something entirely new—a butterfly with a different mode of living—a different way of looking at the world, with wings instead of feet. And so within each of us is built up something called, in occultism, the solar body—a body which will endure throughout the ages when time has passed.

The god within us, that is our real self, our true self. All the lesser things will pass away; but that will, that wisdom, that power which called them into existence can always recall them. All the things of beauty, all the things of joy and happiness—everything that has enthralled the heart of man—those things which belong to his peace are still existent.

We worry about man polluting the planet till it becomes a cosmic dustbin. It will happen if we don't look out. It shouldn't of course; but if it does, still the archetypes of everything that is good, beautiful, and true, are in the mind of the Eternal. And when we take our places as full-grown sons and daughters of the Most High, universe-builders in our own right, then shall we be able to bring back into visible manifestation, in whatever universe we are working, the things of beauty and of joy and peace. Think of it; the destiny of mankind, as occultism perceives it, is to be coworkers with the Eternal.

In the meantime, starting right down here on earth, we can have a lot of fun, because you can get a lot of fun out of occultism. You begin to see your neighbor in a new light, and you get rid of a lot of top-heaviness. Your head decreases in size and you take a smaller size in hats; you learn tolerance; you learn understanding, and, what's more, you learn to have a damn good laugh at yourself.

In the qabalistic teaching there is one angel who stands next to the presence of the Holy One, and he's called the Angel of Mirth and Laughter. A doleful occultist is a misnomer, a contradiction in terms. There ain't no such thing; if he's doleful, he's not a true occultist. The true occultist learns to laugh at himself and not the other fellow. It's all right to see the other fellow slip on a banana skin and go down, but that's a cruel form of amusement. The moment we fall on a banana skin, what a difference in our outlook; we're thinking all kinds of terrible things about the person who . dropped it. So we have to learn to laugh at ourselves, get some fun out of life, not be doleful people, not let our occult gatherings be like a revival meeting. It has to be joyful (I don't say orgiastic—we don't want to go back too far into the past). Worship the Earth

Mother if you like. She is the feminine principle of God, of God Himself. Every power of God has its feminine counterpart, its shakti, as they call it in India. But you don't have to go back to the beastliness of the past; there are new forms to be built, new ways of worshipping the feminine.

In the old days the Great Earth Goddess was worshipped in the Mediterranean as the Great Mother; and the worship of the Great Mother became so foul that when Christianity arose, it repudiated the whole lot because of its vitiation. Even the Romans (and they weren't what you would call a moral people) got fed up with it. Although we don't need to follow those who are trying to revive the dark side of the Earth Mother, we can still acknowledge it as the Great Eternal Manifest of the Father-Mother God, the Chokmah and Binah of qabalah. That also applies to the relationship between the sexes; indeed, it applies to all relationships between groups of people, between countries and nations.

There are traditions which say, "East is East and West is West." You follow whichever you like; but if you were born in the West, the likelihood is that your line of progress is of the Western Mystery Tradition. But it doesn't always follow. Dr. Annie Besant, for instance, was born in the West, but she was a true Easterner. It was in the East that she found her master, and there are others of the East who have found their masters in the West. To every man his own master, and who are you to judge another's servant? To his own master he stands or falls. Remember that; it's one of the fundamental tenets of occultism. You don't have to worry about other people's masters—how they are getting on and whether they're being initiated before you. Oh yes, you can get really peeved about that! Believe me, I've been through it. But if you can keep a level head, and keep it small too, you've a good chance of getting through. I can only say this: In this world, I know of nothing more satisfying, nothing more cheering, nothing more truly helpful than occultism. It has given me insight, knowledge, gnosis—whatever you like to call it. It has enabled me to see myself, more or less, as I really am. It's knocked a lot of the silliness out of me, and I hope it's made me a better person. It's a happy, joyous path, even though on that path we make sacrifices of ourselves. The sacrifice itself is joyous;

even service in the worst quarters can be joyous if the spirit is there.

So don't be disheartened because I've talked of the lords of darkness — the terrible ones we'd like to blast against the wall, those sons of perdition, those wandering stars for whom is reserved the blackness of darkness to the ages of ages. The biggest one of them can be confronted by you and driven away.

But you must think of yourself in the right way. There is danger if you fool around, and I've seen some of it. Still there is perfect safety, perfect happiness and joy if you go about things in the right way — eternal joy and happiness beyond anything we can ever dream or think of. Once or twice in high vision I've been sent into spheres where I've experienced some little part of that joy, as far as I could carry it. And, believe me, the heart of the Eternal is most infinitely kind.

I hope this informal talk will prepare you for the other talks I'm going to give later on. But please believe me when I say what I'm talking about is something I know about. I don't speak about anything I haven't personally experienced. Anybody, a tape recorder, a parrot, can discourse learnedly on the Tree of Life, Chokmah, Binah, and the rest of it till the cows come home. Anybody can do it, if they can talk at all. But it isn't the talk that matters. When I give you the scheme of things, it's so you can put it into practice yourself. See whether it's true, that's the real test. Don't say, "It's true because Mr. Butler says so."

Whatever I tell you is bound to be less than the truth. As a personality I cannot bring through anything which fully explains what I've seen. Even the simple little act of astral projection defies description. I cannot tell you what it feels like to be out there on the astral. I can explain the experience, but I can't give you the gnosis, the absolute knowledge of what it is. You can listen to my words and you can form your own mental picture and you might say, "Well, I don't think the old man's a liar, so that's possibly what happens."

But it isn't what really happens. It's fourth dimensional, and I cannot explain the fourth dimension to you. All I know is that I get pushed into it when I go out on the astral. So there it is. I'm speaking and I'm looking in a mirror darkly. I'm trying to do my best.

You know the old yarn about the Wild West saloon. In it there was a notice over the piano: "Don't shoot the pianist, he's doing his best." So when I talk to you and you find some flaw in what I'm saying, fire back at me; do, for heaven's sake; don't take everything I say lying down. If there's anything you want to contradict or disagree with, come back at me. I don't mind. But don't shoot the poor old pianist, that's all!

Questions from the Floor and Answers

Question: Regarding what you said about uniting the Earth Mother and the subconscious portions of ourselves with the sky portions of ourselves, could you go into this a bit more, as it seemed very abstract to me.

W.E.B.: I was speaking in terms of principles. We talk a great deal about the personality—this thing which we possess, this personality of body, of emotions, of mind that makes a composite whole (sometimes it is called the "quaternary," the four, and includes the *mind,* the *emotions,* the *etheric body,* and the *physical body).* That is the persona, the mask which we're using. Like the actors of old, we speak through the mask of our personality. If our personality booms, then so does our voice. If our voice distorts the meaning of our words, it's because our personality does. But we also have behind us that which we've built up through the ages, a higher personality, an individuality if you like—a place in us where our true I-ness is, where the ego really lives, because the ego which feeds down here in the physical body is a false ego. It's been built up by all our earth experiences, and all of this is built into the personality. It depends upon our birth, upon our circumstances, upon life around us. In the past we've built up personalities of the same type, and the essence of those personalities exists in a higher personality—a higher individual—which is our true individuality, our true I-ness, where our true self is. In that, or shining above it, is the God the Eternal, the sky-force. Our job is to unite this personality, to cleanse it, purify it—to get it straight—and unite it with that individuality. That's our job in life, just to do that.

Question: Is the occult supernatural?

W.E.B.: No. There is nothing supernatural except the Maker of Nature. He, He-She (I don't like using these terms because, grammatically speaking, the male embraces the female, so that when we say "he," we are also saying "she"). So if I say the Eternal is manifested in two aspects—the Father-Mother God—that's one way of putting it. And the only One that is supernatural is the Father-Mother God, the Eternal Being, from Whom and by Whom, everything was made. He is above and beyond, controlling everything He's made. He's the only One Who is supernatural. Everything else obeys laws, the laws of the Eternal, and is natural. This is a natural law in a spiritual world. There is not anything in occultism that is not purely natural. I've seen things levitating in the air. Was this done supernaturally? No, not at all, just according to certain purely natural forces, working by natural law. There is no such thing as supernature, but there is paranormal—above the normal, beyond the ordinary. It isn't everybody that can lift a glass by telekinetic action. Therefore it's paranormal; but at the same time, it's perfectly natural.

Question: There must be part of us which is supernatural.

W.E.B.: Yes, there is that part which is supernatural—the spark of the flame that is eternal within us, and that is supernatural. So we are really supernatural beings in our essence.

Question: And is that the part which we are trying to attain?

W.E.B.: Yes.

Question: Without a teacher or someone to guide you when you wish to serve, how do you know you are serving in truth?

W.E.B.: There is that within you which can give you guidance; there is that inner intuition which can give you the light you seek so long as you're prepared not to jump the gun, so long as you don't try to force your ideas forward, but rely on that inner intuition.

You can use a system of meditation and work on it; it enables you to check things for yourself. Or you can take a simple code of ethics and work with that. Try your best to follow that light. If you do this in all sincerity and truth, after a time (it may be a short time; it may take longer) someone or something will come to you. It may be a book you're reading when suddenly a light flashes in your mind and you see the way in front of you. Sometimes it's a person who comes to you and gives you the same instructions. It happened twice in my lifetime. There was a certain point when I needed to go further, and someone came to me and acted as my teacher. That can happen to you. It can happen to anyone because there's none of us favored, none of us with a hot line to heaven. But if we really work in sincerity and truth and have as much patience as a snake has tail, then ultimately you get started. And once you get started, you proceed by putting one foot in front of the other. Just that. There's no elevator to heaven.

THE
WESTERN TRADITION

The title of my discourse this morning is the "Western Tradition." There's a good deal of nonsense talked about the question of traditions—as if everything were clearcut and all laid down on fixed lines, and we belong to this tradition and that tradition. It's like a lot of other things; it varies tremendously. A person can come into a tradition and go so far in it. Then by a curious concatenation of circumstances they seem to be heaved out on their ear. Usually there's a little bit of trouble as they go, or else they slip out quite unobtrusively without saying a word—just simply drop interest and they're gone. And those who are wedded to a rigid, fixed view are heard to say, "Oh dear, oh dear, why did they do that?" They get quite hot and bothered about the person leaving.

To a great extent, the Eastern and Western Traditions are interchangeable, but the psychology of individuals is different. (You can't lump people together in a mass—except those people who are below a certain level of mental evolution. These you can because they're working as a mass, and you have the crowd mind at work.) But, as individuals begin to seek the way for themselves, they begin to come on to the path. They become individuals, separate people with their own particular lines. They may come to a phase in their evolution when the Western Schools are best for them. But later on, as unseen, deep psychological factors in their souls begin to alter, they begin to veer in another direction. Then they may possibly seek the Eastern Tradition and a guru of some kind. A guru is a teacher, and a guru-chela relationship is part of the Eastern Tradition, whereas in the West you have a different form of teacher-student relationship. The idea is the same; the methods are different.

I'm getting a certain amount of malicious pleasure out of the fact that the East has invaded the West. All those swamis, maharishis, and gurus who were the plague of India have now discovered a good thing in the West.

And to the great horror of those people who have worshipped them, they are starting to cash in on their popularity in the West.

But the Western Tradition has this particular factor in its make-up: There must not be any worship of any person. Personality worship is absolutely out—whether it be Dion Fortune, W. E. Butler, MacGregor Mathers, or Aleister Crowley—it is definitely out if you want to progress. We're trying to get away from the personal element. When you look at some of the occult schools in London and round about in recent years, and you know something about the inside workings, you soon find there's more boiler explosion to the square inch than you ever realized simply because of personality worship. If you're worshipping one personality and I'm worshipping another, we're rival prophets on the scene, and human nature being what it is . . . fights, struggles, take-overs ensue. For that reason the Western Schools try to keep the thing on an individual basis which does not involve dependence on anyone else. It is dependent on the teaching you receive, and this you can sort out for yourself. But it is not, "Thus saith the Lord." If I were trying to teach anyone of you in private, I would say, "Here's an exercise which may help you." I'm duty bound to tell you what the effects of that exercise would be, to tell you how it works as far as I know. Then it's up to you to decide whether it's worth your while following it up. But I must not say to you, "Do this." I can only say, "I would advise you to do this. This is a method which has been found satisfactory, and I think it will apply in your case. Try it!" But I must never say, "You must!"

I want to make that quite clear at the beginning because there's an awful lot of "you must" about. It's something which the Western Tradition has definitely ruled out. There are those from the Western Tradition who, as teachers, have tried the method of force; Crowley did for one and he came unstuck. MacGregor Mathers did and he came unstuck. Dion Fortune did and she nearly came unstuck. We've all experienced it; we've all worked very closely to that particular pit, because it's so easy to. (If you know something and some other poor fellow doesn't, you feel you must unload; you must tell him what to do, and it must be done according to the way in which you received it and which you think is the only way.) The fact of the matter is, "The ways of God are as many as the breaths of the sons of men," as the old Arabic proverb has it. There's plenty of diversity.

Never allow anyone to take you over—whether they call themselves a maharishi, a guru, a mahatma, or an adept. There are a lot of adepts around, a tremendous number of adepts, and they haven't got enough wisdom to button their pants; but there're always some fools to follow them. But remember, sometimes they do a certain amount of good (as I was once reminded and reprimanded by my own teacher).

I was about seventeen at the time, brash and full of my own importance. I had been talking to my teacher, belaboring a certain order, saying, "They're simply after the loot; there's nothing in what they teach." "Right," he said, "let's take this a stage further. That simple teaching is attracting certain followers. Now, would what I give out to you and your colleagues be acceptable to these people?" "No, of course it wouldn't; they couldn't understand it," I answered. He went on, "No they couldn't, but they can understand what they're getting from their own order. It's the right teaching given out in a bad way, but it's working. When those who listen are ready for further knowledge, they will leave that order to seek it. In the meantime, the only people who can help them on the path are those of the order you are denigrating." After that I kept my mouth shut and didn't criticize quite so much.

The Western Esoteric Tradition, as we know it today, is an accumulation of different strains and cultures. It has its roots in the multi-nation Mediterranean basin; Egypt, Greece, Rome, Chaldea, Assyria, and Judea have all contributed to it. So you can be in the Egyptian School or the Chaldean School or the Greek School within the Western Tradition. In the same way you can belong to a different branch of the Eastern Tradition.

It's common to think that Egypt was the source of all the mystic wisdom of the West. I have a great respect for the Egyptian Tradition, but there are others who have expressed equally the secret wisdom to the West—Chaldea for instance. Chaldea and Egypt brought two different streams of knowledge to the common pool, at the same time passing it on to Greece, from whence it went to Rome and to the Near East. It was further enriched by the Judaic Hebrew element and the teaching of the Jewish qabalah, which has become the basis of teaching in all Western Mystery schools. So the Western Tradition has the Egyptian, the Greek, the Hebrew, and the Chaldean lines of succession. A good old jumble, and because of that, because it's a bit of a mongrel, it's a vital thing. Some of the Eastern lines are effete. I've seen them at work in India; they've become effete because they're too inbred. They've kept themselves very close to themselves; they haven't allowed other traditions to influence them, so in the end they've become old hat, out-of-date.

The West has suffered in the opposite way. It's been a kaleidoscope of different influences coming in and out, and there's no real steady school on which you can put your finger and say, "That is the 'Western Tradition.'" We have what Dion Fortune called "a conglomerate" tradition.

When you come into the Western Tradition you're up against a certain system of training, which is the same throughout but slanted in different ways according to the different personalities involved. The Eastern Tradition is more a bulldozing tradition—that is to say, you've got to fit into the system. In the West the system fits itself to you as well as you fitting to it. It's a neutral affair, so there's no hard and fast book of rules. You follow the light as you see it.

Now, if you follow the light as you see it, you may possibly land in some queer patches; but if you're in the tradition, you'll be helped out of them. The way you're taught in the West is by proving the thing for yourself. It's the old system of the apprentice who learns by doing. You don't learn occultism just by reading books—not even mine! You get a lot of information, yes, but a parrot or a tape recorder could just as easily give you that information. Information in itself isn't vital. The vital thing is that through the information you've obtained, you begin to work in the same way as an apprentice.

The apprentice is given a job to do, and the only help the craftsman in charge of him gives is to say, "You know how to file, don't you?" "Yes." "Okay then, get all these bars to the same length and file them square." The poor little apprentice goes to work. He has the minimum amount of information and he's got to put the maximum amount of muscle power into the filing job. He can't understand why and he cusses a bit, "Why should I have to do this; I wanted to make engines." He wanted to do something big; instead, he's set to filing a lot of hard pieces of steel. But he does it, and in the doing he learns to file without blistering his hands. And when he's learned that, he can go a stage further.

So in the Western Tradition it is always a question of going stage by stage, grade by grade. "*Gradus,*" as you probably know, means a step. So a grade is a step forward. You pass through the grades, not necessarily by ceremonial initiations which are nothing but nice little bits of theater—very helpful, very useful if taken in the correct way, but otherwise theater and sometimes very good theater. In the Golden Dawn's[1] early days, Aleister Crowley did a magnificent bit of theater; he took a piece of Golden Dawn ritual and worked it out on the stage for all London to see. One of his leading ladies in the Golden Dawn at that time was Florence Farr, an actress; and she actually went to a ball dressed up in the robes of her Golden Dawn grade. Well, that kind of play acting went too far.

I want to get it into your minds that this business of dolling up and looking like a Christmas tree with all the badges of your degree is not the real thing—although it can be useful, very useful indeed. But mark you, we all make the same mistake sometimes. Shortly after I was initiated into the Inner Light,[2] my wife and I were talking about occultism to some friends who lived on the same street as we. When the talk turned to ritual, I said, "Wait a minute! I've got something I'll show you." I dressed in my robes and proudly showed them off. Now those people weren't initiated; they didn't even belong to a lodge or order of any kind. The next time I went to my own lodge, my chief called me aside and said, "Just a word in your ear: Robes are meant to be worn in private." I got a scolding that I didn't forget and I never made the same mistake again. The tendency is always there. We're all children at heart, and we all do these silly little tricks sometimes—nothing terrible, just foolish.

Now in these grades in the esoteric fraternity there's a lot of nonsense talked about how high you are, how low you are. But you must never think of how low you are; you always must be high, very high. When you come across anyone trying to boast of their position in an order or fraternity, be on your guard. You've either met one of the grownup children who likes to shout and say, "Look how big I am," or else you've got somebody who doesn't understand what he's doing. And they're the dangerous ones. So if someone comes along and says to you, "You're in such and such a group now, which is all right for the average person I suppose; but you're an advanced soul, an old soul. You shouldn't be in that. Now I know of a fraternity where you will get real teaching." That's the bait. "It's only kindergarten stuff," they tell you. "Real teaching is what you want. You're ready for it. I can see that."

It's astonishing how many people fall for that simple little gambit—so simple and yet gold bricks have been sold by the thousand on the strength of it. You're told you have a superior intellect and therefore you will recognize the truth when you see it. So when, a little later on, you're told about gold bricks, you can't let your own superior intellect down by saying it isn't a gold brick. You have to go along with the swindler and get swindled. That is why some very intelligent people get caught with the simplest con tricks. Occultism has too many of what I call psychic and occult swindlers, people who are in it simply for what they can get out of it. It's not occultism; it's skullduggery pure and simple—but very cleverly done. It's applied psychology.

What do you get in a grade then? A grade isn't a question of having passed a certain examination which will allow you to go higher. You've written an essay all about the tree of life. You know all the correspondences of the sephiroth. You've meditated and had funny little visions of elemental beings. So now you're ready for the next grade. But maybe you're not ready for the next grade at all. It could even be you're ready to be demoted and pushed down a grade. What you should be trying to do is not simply to make the personality bigger and more powerful—not that. You're trying to make it better, trying to make it a more efficient instrument, trying to make it something worthwhile—an instrument that will do the work. It doesn't need to be made bigger; it needs quality not quantity.

The thing that brings you into the next grade in the true schools is this. You've developed certain powers (and you can develop them quickly), but what have you done with those powers? How have they affected your life? This is the true test. You're an apprentice who's been fighting like mad for months, but what have you got to show for it? Are you capable of doing greater work? That's the key. What have you done with what you've achieved? It's no use shouting and bellyaching "I want to serve; I want to serve" if you haven't created within yourself the preliminary conditions which will help you to serve. When that apprentice we spoke of has learned to file correctly instead of seesawing his file, he's put on the next job. And when you have learned to do your occult chores correctly, you pass to the next grade automatically. Whether or not you receive ritual initiation into a lodge doesn't matter two hoots. There are people who have never had initiation into any order or any lodge; they wouldn't know the first thing about it, but they have passed high initiations on spiritual levels. There are people who have never joined a fraternity, but who are, nevertheless, highly advanced occultists.

If you do learn your occult chores correctly, you come to the next grade, the next step, and only then is your previous grade completed. You cannot complete a grade until you get to the next one and can look back with a different point of view. You're always doing this in occultism, always being converted. The word "conversion" comes from the Greek word "*metanoia*," and that means to turn round and look at things from a different point of view. As you move into a new grade, you find that there are many things which you have viewed from a certain angle and thought about in a certain way which you now begin to realize weren't correct. It was right for you at the time, but you can never say it will be correct all the time. "New occasions teach new duties. Time makes ancient good uncouth; they (new occasions) must upward still, and onward, who would keep abreast of Truth."[3] You must be abreast in doing, always going forward. That's the point.

In going forward, you can go too fast or you can go too slow. Too slow and things catch up with you with a hefty kick that makes you sit down. If you go too fast, you trip over some obstacle you haven't seen. You have to choose the middle way, a mean between two extremes.

And so we come to that very wonderful system which is the backbone of the Western Tradition, the qabalah. There again, if you think that by reading Z'ev ben Shimon Halevi's books you know it all, then you're wrong. All the books on qabalah, the *Zohar,* the *Sepher Yetzirah,* all the mystic Gematria (and that's a jungle you can quickly lose yourself in) all that isn't what matters. It's the relationships behind it that are important. Don't worry about whether you can remember if it's "Geburah" or "Gedulah," "Pachad" or "Chesed," or whatever. "Hesed," of course, is spelt "Chesed"; that "C" in the Hebrew is silent. The same with "Hockmah/Chokmah." If you have a little bit of Hebrew it helps, but it's not necessary. If anyone asked me, "What's the Hebrew name for the thirty-second path?" I'm damned if I could tell you offhand. And I've been at it for sixty-odd years. It's not really necessary; but if you can manage it, it's helpful. It's better than having to scratch your head or refer to a book. When you're fighting, you don't carry a lot of extra equipment about with you. You remove everything that gets in the way, so you can fight lightly. In this fight—and it is a fight—you don't clutter yourself up with a lot of extra baggage.

This brings me to another point. I want to give you some idea of how we go about training pupils or apprentices in the Western Tradition. The idea is not to fill you up with factual information but to present you with a way of thinking. You see the difference? A way of thinking so that you look at things from a different point of view. That's really what it's all about. When you have that, you get away from a personal viewpoint—very slowly to begin with, often with a lot of trouble, but eventually you manage it. Then you begin to perceive that your former point of view was illusory; you were entranced by the glamour; you've been asleep and now you're beginning to wake up. There was one great occultist who maintained that the whole of humanity was sleepwalking. That was Gurdjieff. The ones that come on the path are the ones who have awakened from sleep. Have you ever observed a London crowd walking along the street? They're staring in front of them, not a smile on their faces, tearing along as if the very devil's after them. There's a kind of strained look on their faces as if they're absolutely lost. Here and there you see somebody having a smile—so rare it's the kind of exception that proves the rule.

Now we all do that because we've created within ourselves a set of automatic actions. We do things in a particular way and we get set in that way. We get up at a certain time and do certain things always in the same way. We have dinner at a fixed time every evening, lunch at the same time, and so on. Habit becomes so rigid the stomach responds accordingly. If you try to make a change, there's trouble; your stomach begins to protest because you're upsetting the pattern. Your mind acts in the same way. It gets set in mental habits. We look at things through spectacles we've created for ourselves, spectacles with colored lenses instead of clear glass. We see everything through the lens of our own personality. It may be blue or green, red or ginger; very rarely is it crystal clear. W. T. Stead[4] called mediumistic communications "stained glass," because the mind of the medium stained and altered the communication as it was filtered through the meshes of the mental concept of the medium. In the same way, everything which comes through from the inner planes to you is colored by the personality which you have built.

The whole essence of esoteric training is the rebuilding of the personality. You can begin when you're ninety and you can begin when you're nine. I started when I was nine. That's when I had my first occult experience; it was a real humdinger, really out of this world. I'll tell you the story. It's interesting; it shows you how things that draw you towards the occult sometimes work.

I was a small boy in a little Yorkshire village—way back, 1909 or thereabouts. Life was very simple in the village—getting up, working, and going to bed again. Because I was ill most of the time and had very little education, I used to read a lot to make up for it. One day I got hold of a magazine which carried an account of a magical evocation. As I read it, my ears flapped. This was it! I knew nothing about occultism at the time. You wouldn't have dared to mention the word in the village in those days.

I thought, I'm going to have a go at this. I was always a believer in trying things out (blew my eyebrows off several times while making gunpowder!). Anyway, having read the article, I thought, here we go! And one Saturday morning I went into the woods near our village to a place called "the Planting." In the valley at the bottom of the woods was a tumulus of some old British chieftain. It seemed to me at the time to be the ideal place for my experiment, hidden and well away from everybody. So I set forth with paper and matches. I climbed to the top of the tumulus with my book of words, lit the paper, and fed it odds and ends of firewood from the surrounding wood.

It was a brilliant clear summer morning, not a cloud in the sky. As the fire got going, I started doing my stuff. As I read aloud the words of the evocation, a kind of veil came down blotting out the sun. At first I didn't notice it and thought the sun had gone behind a cloud. But no, the sun was still there; something seemed to be getting in the way. I couldn't tell what it was. It seemed as if my eyesight was going. The veil became thicker and thicker until there was fog all round me and I couldn't see either the sun or the surrounding place at all. I began to get scared; I was lost. If you've ever been lost in a fog you'll know that feeling of helplessness. You don't know which way to go to get out of it, and I didn't know whether to stay, jump off the mound, or what. But you reach a certain point when you get so frightened, you can't get frightened any more; and this happened to me. Nine years old I was, standing on top of a tumulus surrounded by fog in the middle of a bright summer's day. But in that fraction of a second of freedom from fear, I made my decision. I simply rolled off the top of that tumulus like a shot rabbit; I rolled over and over till I reached the bottom. Immediately I was back again in brilliant sunshine, no sign of fog; everything was normal except I was sweating and feeling very, very scared. It took me several days to get over it, but I'd learned something there. It didn't put me off trying again; it simply whetted my appetite. That kind of thing happens to a lot of people; they find themselves drawn to occultism in devious ways which then lead them on to other things. I was attracted to what the spiritualists call materializations. I've seen some extraordinary psychic phenomena in my time.

One evening, a long time ago, I looked up to the platform where someone was speaking and I thought, I know that man. When he came down from the platform, I cornered him and said, "I want to speak to you." He looked at me for a few moments, then said, "Yes, of course, we've met before." He gave me an address in London to go to, and that was how I met my first teacher. From him I learned the rudiments of magic. With his aid, I went out of the body for the first time and learned something of the reality behind life. Later on, by another thread of curious circumstances, I met Dion Fortune and joined her group. All along there has been that direction. If you're really on the path—and it's not just a way of passing the time, something new to do—if you're truly serious and prepared to take whatever comes, then that certain door will open for you as it did for me. As the old Eastern adage has it, "When the pupil is ready, the teacher appears." And it's true enough, but the teacher may not be a turbanned Hindu or a grave-looking Egyptian priest or anyone like that. It's more likely to be someone in jeans who chats with you and suddenly says something which opens your eyes, gives you insight, and alters your course of direction. It may be that through that person you meet your teacher; it may also be through you that others meet their teacher. That's the way it goes.

I've given you this talk about the Western Tradition and I don't seem to have said much; but, if you think out the implications, you'll find it goes quite a long way. I've tried to give an idea of the Western Tradition, not as a stereotyped school of occultism, but rather as a workable method of reacting to life itself. It may be grading in schools, in fraternities, or you may choose to go your own lone way. Whichever path you choose, it's the method that counts. If you use methods of the Western Mystery Tradition, then just as surely as when you pick up the telephone, dial, and make contact with someone on the other end, you will get in touch with those who matter, who stand behind the tradition: The Invisible Lodge, that great company on the inner planes who are the real masters and the true teachers. But you have to go to them, and they will come to you if you make the conditions right. You have to ring them because they're not necessarily going to ring you unless somewhere or other in your karma it is necessary for you to meet them. Even though you meet them and they help you, there are dozens of other people who meet them and don't receive any help because they're not open to it. But, if you're ready, the teacher will appear and the way ahead be made open to you.

Once you get that guidance and teaching, you'll find it is in tune with and is supported by your inner teaching—that is, intuition, teaching from within. But the teaching from within must balance with the teaching from without. Otherwise you'll be so full of knowledge you'll have to be carried about in a truck; your head will be so big (like those lunar people with heads six feet across that H. G. Wells wrote about) and you'll have no wisdom at all. But if you seek wisdom, then you'll be given it, but you always pay for what you get. "You never get nowt for nowt and very little for sixpence," as the Yorkshire saying has it. You've got to work for it, and then it comes to you in all kinds of different ways; but it comes. I can testify that in over sixty years' experience, again and again, it has come. It's never pushed on you. The Lord doesn't empty a bucket of golden sovereigns on top of your head. But when you've made the conditions right, then it will come. Occasionally in the past you've made conditions and other things have come, things you didn't want perhaps. Somewhere in the past I made a slip, and the result is I'm now a disabled person with four different kinds of trouble. I could easily moan, "Why should this happen to me?" I could easily say that. Instead I simply say, "Because it's happened, there's a reason, a purpose to it; therefore, stop grumbling and get on with it."

That's the way in which the initiate in the West faces life. He doesn't try to make excuses for himself; he tries to understand the law and work with it and accept that which comes to him whether of good or ill. I'm not saying you have to go down under it, but accept it and then begin to work it out.

"Through wisdom is a house built; and by understanding it is established," says the qabalistic verse in the Bible.[5] By wisdom and understanding. If you get understanding and you follow it up with wisdom, wisdom says this: Know, will, dare, and keep silent. Know, will, dare—yes, dare—don't be afraid of things. Dare, but keep silent. When anybody tells me they'd been raising elementals in the back garden last night, I take that with a considerable amount of salt. If they really did it, they would keep quiet about it.

Questions from the Floor and Answers

Question: I was interested in what you said about the invasion of the West by the gurus of the East. Could you enlarge on why you think this has happened?

W.E.B.: It's happened because of the poverty of the West with regard to these things. Orthodox Christianity has been to blame in many ways, plus the materialistic, deterministic attitude of science. The Victorian scientists, who were so sure they knew the atom could not be divided, have had to take a reef in their sails because the atom has been divided and subdivided and subdivided again. They're talking about tachyons now, and they have no relation to electrons or protons; they're a kind of semi-psychic background to matter; and the physicists are beginning to talk in these terms. The idea of natural selection, the Darwinian hypothesis of the evolution of species, has undergone a complete revolution. If anyone talks to you in terms of Edward Clodd's books on evolution or H. G. Wells' ideas, they're absolutely old hat, out-of-date. The modern evolutionist has, again, to take a reef in his sails because new facts have emerged which have altered his ideas altogether. For instance, we now know that mutations, sudden alterations in species, can take place through radiation. Darwin and his friend Wallace knew nothing of that. We know that mutations can take place very rapidly, there again altering the time scale. Until a few years ago, we thought we knew all about radiocarbon dating, a method to determine how old an artifact is. Now we find it is not so accurate. They can't pin it down as they thought they could but have to do their homework all over again.* The whole concept is changing. Even Einstein's theory of relativity has had to be modified.

The deterministic attitude of science has gummed up real scientific work with paranormal things. I read an account the other day of a very prominent scientist, and this is what he said, "Even though I received indubitable evidence that this happened, I would not believe it because, to me, it is impossible." That's a scientist, and he's an honest scientist. There are many others who are not so honest; but there it is.

Because of that, the prevailing intellectual climate has become purely materialistic. But the East hasn't had to contend with this form of materialism, so now the East is beginning to feed into the

---

* Since this lecture was delivered in 1978, the former validity of carbon dating has been restored with slight modifications.

vacuum created in the West. At the same time, the West is feeding into a similar vacuum in the East that has been brought about by its acceptance of the doctrine of reincarnation. The doctrine of reincarnation has been the greatest curse of the East, leaving people to take what comes. "Oh it's my karma," they say and lie down under it and let themselves be submitted to oppression and starvation. I've seen them lying in the streets of Calcutta, dying for lack of food while rich Hindus walked past them because "It's my karma! I mustn't fight against my karma." And so reincarnation wrongly understood has been one of the greatest curses of the East.

Now they're being fed with the materialistic ideas of the West. Now they've been told, "We're improving your hygiene; we have community schemes going; we find wells and dig them; we're making all sorts of improvements. You don't need to suffer like this. It isn't your karma." I remember hearing someone talking about healing in India, saying, "This healing interferes with a man's karma." Dr. Annie Besant, president of the Theosophical Society answered, "Try putting it this way. If the man is healed, then it's evident it is his karma to be healed." So in that way, increasingly, the East is learning from the West.

Remember the doctrine of reincarnation is very complex, and when taken by the average person simply to mean the reincarnation of this personality, then it's ruinous. It can breed trouble—left, right, and center. Now the West is doing a splendid job for the East, but it has only touched the fringe of the problem. The mystic East is still the light from the East, but the West has its own light and the two together can illuminate the world.

Question: You were talking just now about science and those things. I find it difficult to interpret scientific findings. They don't seem to fit in with the teachings of the occult or of Christianity.

W.E.B.: The point is this: The scientist is not trying to prove or disprove anything other than the truth; that's what he's after. He tells you he's searching for the truth, but he's biased. He has a personality that is slanted in various ways, and to some people keeping the good opinion of a neighbor counts largely above truth. So he's liable to stretch the truth a little, give it the odd twist here and there. Then again, he's looking at things from a different point of view; the goal of his experiment is to determine whatever he can determine and then to see if it is repeatable. If it can be repeated again and again, then he reckons there must be some law underlying it because the same conditions always bring about the same result. So the scientist deduces a working hypothesis and the means to apply it in that particular field of research. Should another fact emerge which contradicts his first lot of facts, he has somehow to include it. You can't get rid of a fact; it's there, solid, so it has to be accommodated into the system. If the system won't accommodate the fact, the system goes to blazes and the scientist has to devise a new system. That's the way in which science works.

Religion works by having a predetermined idea and you work from that. The facts have then to fit into the predetermined idea. It's a reversal, but if the two can work together, then you get something worth having. There are scientists who do work that way— they get a sudden intuition—like Tesla and Edison and one or two others. They intuit a certain concept which has no fact to stand upon at all, no fact which proves it or supports it. But that flash of inspiration drives them on. They go to work to find the facts which will give credence to it in the world of men. It's astonishing how they do it. They're working from above downwards, and the conventional scientist is working from below upwards. Both have their respective parts to play, and the true balance is when you get the spiritual scientist who takes both worlds into account and doesn't get stuck in either.

Question: The thing that worries me is the fact that they say they have created new life, albeit life that only lasts for a millionth of a second.

W.E.B.: Well, put it this way: Life has appeared, but have they created it? They've created the conditions under which life can manifest. In the same way if I, in a dry room, rub a piece of fur on a piece of ebonite, I create the conditions for an electrical discharge. If I put my finger near it, I've "made" static electricity, but I haven't really made it; it was already there. No one makes force. The force is always there beforehand, but as with this latest lark, we can create the right conditions for force to manifest. They say they've made life in a test tube, but half the work has been carried out with living tissue. All they're saying is "Life has appeared" where they didn't expect it to be. That only means life is ubiquitous. Give the right conditions, and it oozes through. It's a living Universe, not a dead one. But this is one way in which the scientist can square his conscience with what is happening. Many scientists are wanting to go this way but cannot because their old conceptions of what is natural science have to be torn down. Supposing someone attacks my very belief that there is something beyond this world; immediately I react by saying it doesn't matter because I know. But if they bring proof after proof which seems to contradict what I believe, there comes a point at which I begin to waver. Immediately I get furious in defense; people do when they are defending what they believe to be truth.

Truth is quite all right. She can look after herself. She may reside at the bottom of a well with nothing on; but as the Bible says, "Great is truth and Mighty above all things."[6]

Training the Personality:

THE RUBBISH
IN THE BACK ROOM

If you look around Britain today, there are all manner of occult schools, orders, and fraternities. If you read the advertisement pages of *Prediction,* you'll find all sorts of people advertising funny things, and there are some very funny things, too, believe me—and in America even some weirder ones. I had a correspondence with one group which fairly shook me. I'm a staid, old, respectable parson and it shook me solid. It was from an association which reputed to form itself into groups of six, and the six have to be three ladies and three gentlemen, each group a complete element in itself. No question of them having to be husband and wife, or anything like that. It's a common sex group with everything in common, including sex. It shook me up completely because I'm still very orthodox morally. Well, they wanted me to join them. I didn't know whether it was for my prowess or my reputation, but I had to decline the invitation.

Seriously speaking though, there are a great many people organizing occult groups along do-it-yourself lines. Now there's no reason why anyone shouldn't have a go at doing-it-yourself, providing they take the necessary precautions. If you were to set out to wire your own house by do-it-yourself methods, you would take a great deal of care. You would probably get yourself a reliable textbook on the subject, consult anybody you could get hold of with a knowledge of wiring, and even then you could hit a spot of trouble. But, if you went blindly at it, you would most likely have your house on fire within a fortnight. So it is with do-it-yourself occultism. You can do a great deal for yourself, but you can also reach a point where you confuse yourself and mess up the whole thing—burn your fingers and land next door to the loony bin.

Many people think that the Western Tradition and occultism means joining an order or fraternity, like Ibis Fraternity or whatever. But it simply means getting together in a group and forming a group mind. The psychology of the group mind is a governing factor; remember that, because the group mind is a very great influence in occultism.

There are two kinds of groups: a contacted group and a noncontacted group or study group. A study group is useful for pooling ideas and getting new insights because everyone looks at a subject from a different angle. In being exposed to these various points of view, you are helped by participating in such a group. But as soon as a group starts to develop with a committee and begins to delegate authority, trouble starts. Human nature being what it is, somebody else wants to be boss. They're sure they can do it better than the person who is already the boss. They're convinced they've been divinely appointed to do that. They've had a message or a dream from the inner planes which tells them to take over the group because Mrs. So-and-so who is currently running it doesn't know what she's doing. On the strength of that, they go to one or two people who are a little dissatisfied (there's always someone dissatisfied in a group) and enlist their sympathy, stir things up a little. Before you know where you are, you've got a lovely little conspiracy on your hands; and, after about six months, the group suddenly explodes with violence. Either both contenders for leadership go to pieces, or one is subdued and the other raised. I've seen it happen in a hundred cases during my lifetime in this movement.

It's simply human nature, nothing more than that, but it's human nature taking advantage of occult clichés. They talk about messages from the inner planes when what they really mean is a little bit of their own imagination taking hold. You can get plenty of messages from the inner planes if you just sit down and let your mind race away on its own. "Oh, yes," you say, "I'm sure that's a message from the inner planes. It agrees with what I'm thinking."

Thus the noncontacted group is always in danger of splitting up at any given time. By noncontacted, I mean this: A group can either be free, working on its own, an ordinary study group, or it can be ritually, ceremonially, or otherwise linked up with another group on the inner planes. Then it becomes a contacted group. Between the two there's the same difference as between chalk and cheese. The contacted group has authority behind it, but even so you can still get trouble arising sometimes because the head of the group may determine that everything she gets from the inner planes is gospel truth and anything that anybody else gets isn't. And that's personality getting in the way. Nevertheless the contacted group has a definite force, a power behind it which is not merely that of the group mind—of all of the members' minds grouped together. You sit in a group and the subconscious part of your mind links up with the subconscious of the next person's and so on until your group is one subconscious mind, and that *group mind* can be very powerful. Sometimes it happens spontaneously. I'll give you a case in point.

A considerable time ago there was a sultan of Turkey who had the charming nickname of Abdul the Damned. He was altogether a nasty piece of work. Some of the massacres he perpetrated on the Armenians made shocking reading, added to which he had the reputation of indulging in some very dubious practices in his harem. Well, he came to England to visit royalty and drove in an open carriage through London. A group of clerks and office workers were standing watching the carriage go by when, suddenly, somebody raised a shout of "Abdul the Damned." The crowd took it up and within five minutes the police had to interfere in force to rescue old Abdul from being lynched. He was within an inch of being torn to pieces by those inoffensive city clerks who wouldn't normally say "boo" to a goose. But under the influence of the mob mind, they could kill.

Today, we have this business of "rent a crowd." If you want a really good demonstration and have the money at your disposal, you can hire a crowd to shout for you—a senseless chanting, a beating rhythm. It's what the Easterns call a mantra, and it produces an effect by affecting the deep subconscious levels of the minds of the crowd, linking them together in a common emotion. Because of the mob mind, an individual who would not normally hurt another could help lynch a person. As a group, the lowest elements of the subconscious seem to link together. That's a case of the group mind working wrongly.

I'll give you another instance. One of the heroes of the First World War came to London to be received in state. His name was synonymous with victory for our people. He too was driven through London in an open carriage. Suddenly the mob rose up; and, if the police hadn't intervened, he would have been taken from his carriage and carried shoulder-high through the streets of London by the crowd. Again you see irrational, unreasoning blind emotion, but on the good side this time. All the same, if too many people took part in the celebration, they could easily have choked him to death. That's the kind of thing that happens. So if you join an order, fraternity, or group, you have this group mind behind you. In times of distress it can be very helpful because of its telepathic power. Remember that the group mind is telepathic; minds are linking with each other throughout. That's why it spreads so quickly.

There's presently a great deal of study going on in occult lodges about the limits and power of the group mind. When you join a group and the group mind doesn't agree with your mind, one of two things has to happen: Either you go out on your ear, or else you are conquered by the group mind. When you join any fraternity, you lose a certain amount of free will; but you join voluntarily. It isn't forced upon you; no one in the true Mysteries says, "You must!" They simply advise you; and, if you determine you will be linked in that way, then you will be. That's the better side of it. But you can come into collision with the group mind and then, very painlessly, you are edged out. You don't know why or how; you begin to lose interest; certain things cease to appeal to you; you get fed up. It's a wet night so you don't think you'll go to the lodge tonight, and so on. Gradually you slip out, and that's what the group mind wanted. Telepathically you've been turned out of the group.

On the other hand, if you can be of help to the group you'll be drawn in. You have a curious kind of fascination; you feel you want to do more for the group, become part of it and so on. That again is the group mind drawing you into itself. There is always this coming and going. Members of the group are subject to these two forces. If it is a true group, then it's tuning you in all the time to the higher levels. But a personality with all its faults and imperfections doesn't always like that and rebels against it. And in that rebellion you often find the group mind decides that for the good of the rest of the group it's better that the rebel should go. So you're never certain when you get into a group whether you're going to stay there or not.

Take the history of the Golden Dawn. You'll find that people joined and left continuously. There were all kinds of dissensions and rebellions. There was the Crowley rebellion, the Yeats rebellion, the Brodie-Innes rebellion. People seemed to come apart at the seams because of the tremendous forces which played upon them. Their personalities couldn't readjust. It is not a light thing to join any fraternity or order; your personality has to change in the process.

When you come to think about it, we've been building our personality from our earliest days—more by chance than anything else. For instance, if it was our mother who mostly looked after us and we saw very little of our father because he worked away from home, we have a bias towards our mother and against our father. As we grow older, and if we are girls, there is the tendency to seek the mother image because the father image has been lost to us. Or it may be the other way round and the father image is prominent. Whether it's the father image or the mother image, our early experience can create quite a lot of trouble because when we reach the stage at which we are potentially and fully capable of becoming parents, our attitude towards the opposite sex has been determined by those early childhood experiences. So if we're a man with a mother-fixation, we subconsciously choose a woman who will mother us. Then, of course, when she develops an idea of her own that wasn't mother's, we begin to wonder if our pet dog has bitten us. A man who has depended on his mother, relied on her for everything, is going to transfer that reliance to the women of his choice; she has to be a substitute mother to him. Because of this confused father/mother image in the very early days of our childhoods, there's endless psychological trouble that leads to battered babies and other nastiness.

As we grow, similar things happen to us haphazardly on the way, and we build into our temple of the personality all kinds of rough and unsuitable material. Sometimes we get a good brick, square and true, and it builds in very nicely. Another time it's an odd, misshapen chunk of rock and we put that in too. But this chunk makes a very poor foundation for later on; it's liable to come apart at the joints.

Now, because of that haphazard foundation we've built, we arrive at maturity with a very curious temple of the personality: the doors are where the windows should be; the windows are out at the back somewhere; the chimney comes out the side of the house— all kinds of defects. And, if we think we've built a lovely personality—that we are the norm of what a man or woman should be— we are not being honest with ourselves. The temple we've built is a long way from perfect.

When we come into the occult movement and begin our occult work, the first thing we have to do is to get rid of the rubbish built into our temple. We have to remake our foundations. That means we have to work on it while we're still living in it. If you've ever experienced that process in actual life, say, for instance, having a foundation wall put in while you're still living in the house, you'll know what chaos is all about. But it has to be done; we have to be ruthless. That particular rock we've built into our personality, that we're so very attached to—that lovely piece of rock—beautiful, isn't it? Yes, but it's not in the right place; it's not the right material, so out with it.

You have to go through a period, which is the same in both mystic and occult paths; it is called purgation. A purging out, a removing from yourself of those elements which you have built and which are of no further use. Some of them might have been useful when you were young, but they are so much dead wood now. Now you're coming on the path. It feels like getting rid of your heart's blood—innocent things that once were good but are no longer right for you. There's a great deal of hidden teaching in the parable of the "Slaughter of the Innocents" at the birth of the

Christ. When the Christ is born in you, then the innocents very often have to suffer for it; they have to go and it breaks your heart to have to let them go.

On the other hand, once you've done that and you've set the squared and true stones in place and your temple becomes steady on a good foundation, then you perceive that what you did—getting rid of all that rubbish that was no longer any use—was the right thing to do.

There's no wishy-washy emotionalism in occultism. If you think you can get away with a glorious burst of sentimental statements, then you're wrong. Occultism is as true a science as chemistry or electricity. And that is also true of the asceticism which is practiced by some occult orders. It's not a question of repressing the flesh or anything like that. It's simply this: if you're doing one thing, then you cannot do something else that gets in the way of your doing it. There are times when you have to deny yourself that which you would like to do simply because, for the work you are doing, it's incompatible. That is something we all have to learn.

Discrimination is the first virtue on the path. If you go blindly into an order without discriminating, then you're going to run into trouble—no matter who's the head of the order. But if you discriminate, then you find either you're not fit for the order (so you bottle your pride and go away, perhaps to see what you can do to make yourself fit) or else you come into the order prepared to change yourself as you go along. In either case, discrimination is absolutely necessary.

Discretion is also important because discretion and discrimination are the twin virtues of the path. The symbol for discrimination is a little dagger which you carry with you ceremonially in the lodge. Symbolically a critic uses a dagger to tickle something out. He inserts something sharp, twists it around and takes out just what he wants. He pulls out the innards of your beautiful book and then tears it to shreds. And you don't like it one little bit. But criticism is necessary, constructive criticism of yourself. Criticism goes with the discrimination which is in itself a form of criticism.

The image of a key is the symbol for discretion. Remember, discretion and discrimination are the two first virtues of the path. If you acquire those two, never mind whether you can travel on the astral or see things round the corner. Those are incidentals. If you can learn discretion and discrimination, you've built into your personality, your character, two sterling virtues which will be of inestimable value as you tread the occult path.

We come into occultism searching for something; we come seeking, looking for a way forward. What we're really looking for is Eden, the lost Eden where everything was idyllic and beautiful. Adam and Eve living peacefully together in the garden, that's what we're seeking. This is a reflection of that "supernal Eden," as the qabalists call it, which lies far beyond in the spiritual world from which we came. We're looking for an Eden and we look for it in curious ways. We write about it, we sing songs ("Home Sweet Home; Be it ever so humble there's no place like home"). But when we come to analyze it, home is an intangible ideal. You can have a home on the edge of the Gobi Desert and be quite at home there if it's home for you. But, for another person, it might be hell, not home. We're searching all the time for that inner home, so we write songs about it, or we write books like *City of the Sun*,[1] and *Erewhon*.[2] (Read "erewhon" backwards and we get "nowhere.") We're struck will all kinds of ideas, back to ancient Atlantis,[3] for instance, where we feel we must at one time have had all manner of wonderful things. Read the records of Atlantis and you'll find that a lot of people didn't have happy times; nevertheless, for some people it is a dream of a retreat into happiness.

All the time, unconsciously, we're going back to the womb where we were perfectly happy, where everything was done for us. We didn't need to do a thing; we simply lived there. Don't forget psychologists and psychiatrists are discovering that the unborn child isn't entirely unconscious. It's a living being and experiences a certain amount of absolute consciousness before its birth. It can react to certain things, events and impressions, which are imprinted on the mind of the unborn embryo and reappear in later years.

So we're trying to get back to the womb where everything was beautifully peaceful. But that again is only the physical analog of that wonderful womb of creation from which we came. Everything was peaceful in that world, but somehow or other we got kicked out of it. We've come right away from it. Like the prodigal son going out into the far country, we've landed ourselves in a lovely mess and we long to get back. We write yearningly about the City of the Sun; we write learnedly about Atlantis. We try to discharge our emotional longing, our homesickness. St. Augustine put it very aptly: "Lord, Thou hast made us for Thyself, and the heart of man is restless till it finds its rest in Thee."[4] That is the urge; that is the quest which every member of humanity is engaged in. We're trying to find our way back home.

In occultism we've found a way to do it, a way which gives results. The trouble in the West is that orthodox religion has failed to do so. It's become a system of morals, but not a system that gives results. Although to be fair, in a few cases it does. It's a means whereby people can link up with reality, but in the majority of cases it becomes a kind of lip service. It's linked with mores which become morals. Mores are the customs and habits of a tribe, and at different times, the tribe has different habits. Whereas it was good and righteous at one time for you to eat your grandmother, it is equally wrong now for you to eat her. The mores have changed because they are not absolute; they're relative. They depend upon culture and surroundings, education or the lack of it.

Now your mores have got to stand up to the tests of experience and very often your mores—your morals—don't. Apart from that, new occasions bring new duties. As King Arthur says in Lord Tennyson's poem—

> *The old order changeth, yielding place to new,*
> *And God fulfils Himself in many ways,*
> *Lest one good custom should corrupt the world.*[5]

So when you talk about morality or immorality, you have to tread very carefully. But there are eternal values, values which are not in time or space, and they determine true morality. And you can learn these values in occultism as you do in true religion. This morality is simply based upon two things: Right relationship with the source of all life and a right relationship with all life. So you can never do your neighbor a bad turn; you can't abuse your neighbor in any way; you can never turn away from the life which is in all things.

These are two true and eternal laws which are the background of all occultism. The moment anyone talks about having sexual orgies in order to be able to do this, that, and the other—the moment they say that—they show that they are not truly on the path, because they are injuring other people and themselves. And we have no right to injure others or ourselves. We are one with all life, and we do not gain spiritually by ill-treating any other form of life. So if anyone dangles the bait of sex in any form to you as an incitement to join a lodge, the answer is, "Don't!" I've seen some of it; what's more I've had to deal with the wrecks from that kind of abuse. They've come to me and said, "What can I do? I'm a victim of blackmail and I can't get out of it. I'm held in this lodge (or order) and they won't let me go." And I've had to go and sort it out because that was my job. At the same time, it's not an easy mission helping people out of messes of that kind.

So if you're searching for the good, the beautiful, and the true, you don't go looking for the ugly things. "Two men look out through the same bars: one sees the mud, and one the stars."[6] Those things which are good and beautiful in themselves, as sex should be, can become impure and even evil if they are misused. All the good and beautiful things of life can so easily be perverted and fouled if we let our personality get in the way.

Now, let's see what happens when a person joins a lodge and eventually comes before the altar of sacrifice to be initiated (*ab initio* means from the beginning, from the inception), to take the first step. As a candidate he's dressed in white (from *candidus,* meaning white) to signify he's come into something entirely new. But that doesn't mean to say he's become any different from what he was before. When you come to initiation, you bring everything that you are—warts and all—nothing more. Being initiated simply means that you are linked in with cosmic forces; everybody at the ceremony is waiting to turn on the switch. Now when that switch is turned on and those forces begin to work through you, the effect can be drastic, sometimes catastrophic, if your personality hasn't been built to carry the load. When these forces begin to flow, we must have some means of bringing them down to earth, literally to earth. Every occult exercise, if it's properly carried out, will always end by bringing you back, right down to earth. You don't leave yourself in the air. When the rite is finished we make the necessary banishing signs or pentagrams. We stamp on the floor or sound the knells to assert symbolically that we're back to earth, that we've earthed the forces and can now go about our everyday work. Otherwise, if those forces remain with us because of not being properly earthed, they have the effect of making us dreamy, semi-disassociated, and we run into trouble, all kinds of trouble, simply because we haven't earthed ourselves properly.

It's the personality that's likely to cause you trouble when you begin your occult training. Remember how in *Alice in Wonderland* when they played croquet with sticks of living flamingos: every time they ventured to hit the ball the flamingo turned its head the other way, and of course, they didn't get along very fast. Our personality is just like that—a wriggling little thing that doesn't like being trained—it hates training, and the more you try to train it, the more it tries to wriggle out of it. It can't be said too often: The first part of occult training is personality training. You have to delve into your personality, find out what makes it tick. That means self-analysis, and that's hard work.

Say you determine to start with the daily salutes to the sun: one in the morning ("Hail to Thee, the Eternal Spiritual Sun, Whose visible Symbol rises now in the Heavens. Hail unto Thee from the Abodes of Morning."), a similar salute at noon, and the evening or late evening salute. Then you make up your mind that at the end of each day you will go back over that day and look at everything you've done, whether you did the right things, what your motives were, etc. You will go back from your very last action of the day to the first. What happens? You started off full of enthusiasm and good intentions, but by the second or third day, the personality says, "Blow this; this is becoming too uncomfortable." So you sit down to your meditation and half way through it, you're asleep; your personality has just put you to sleep because it didn't like worrying about what you've done and what you haven't done. That's automatic consciousness working without your volition. And, if you persist, it will even give you a headache; you will wake up in the mornings feeling half dead. Then you think, "O Lord, there's something wrong with me! Perhaps the meditation is not suiting me." No, the meditation's suiting you all right, but it's biting the personality and the personality doesn't like it.

Don't forget, it's a child personality; don't get the idea you've lost your childhood. That personality you had as a child is still in you, and if we regress you hypnotically to the age of five, we can find you there. If you were to write while under hypnosis, you would form the same childish letters, use the same expressions. For all intents and purposes, it would be a child of five we're talking to, with a child's understanding. It's living there within you. It has its tantrums; and if it gets half a chance, it can display its tantrums and upset the whole of your adult personality. We're full of contradictions, full of bits and pieces from the past. Because of that, you always have to watch out when you're meditating or concentrating on any occult work that you bring the whole of your personality to it. You don't allow little bits of your personality to trip you up as it will try to do if you don't watch out.

You try meditating at a certain time each day and try to keep a record of your meditations, and I bet you that at the end of six months, you'll find there are lots of entries showing you didn't meditate at the right time, missed it altogether or gave all manner of excuses for not meditating. But, when you boil down the excuses, you will find half of them are simple rationalizations, little lies to yourself: I didn't feel well; I was expecting the maid; I had an unexpected visitor; and so on. Always an alibi. We can give ourselves alibis till the cows come home and kid ourselves that we're meditating, that we're really doing the work. But we are doing nothing more than causing inconveniences to the little bits of ourselves down below, those complexes that are racing around down there. We're doing very little in the way of true meditation. It is better to meditate for five minutes and really mean it—really get down to it—than to do a drifty, dreamy meditation of half an hour, at the end of which you find you are asleep.

I've gone through that phase. We all have at some time or another. I'm not talking from an angle of superiority. It's something we've all done. I don't think there is anyone who has meditated consistently for a year who couldn't put his hand on his heart and say, "What the old boy's saying now is absolutely correct; I've done the same thing." We slip up because that's the way our personality tries to conquer us. It doesn't like being told to do things. It prefers to do everything in its own way, because of that false ego we've built up—the false I, which is not the true ego at all. At one time or another, we have to get rid of that false ego, and we can do this by using its own power in the same way a good wrestler uses the strength of his opponent in order to trip him up.

The whole method of dealing with the personality is one of the occult secrets. Yet there's no "secret" really, just application. It's a system you can use without danger to yourself, but with a lot of pain to that personality of yours, because it cuts it down to size. But you have to do it if you're going to make the personality worth anything. If you're going to use it as an instrument in the hands of your true self, it needs to be sharp at the edges, well-made, strong and powerful, and capable of doing the work you want it to do. You have to take Brother Ass and train him, and you can do that through the system of meditation, concentration, and illumination which is to be found within all true occult teachings.

In that lodge or group of yours, you have polarities. They are magnetisms, vital forces which come from each one of you and make up the combined atmosphere in the group. You can feel the atmosphere; it's almost tangible; and if you don't feel it, then you know there's nothing much doing. In that atmosphere, governed as it is by the common pool of telepathy, those forces begin to work upon your inner senses, upon your chakras, and then your supernormal powers start to unfold. There can be a bit of trouble when one of you thinks he isn't unfolding as quickly as someone else in the group. There's suspicion and mistrust, but it's all part of the growth of the group and the personality. But, if you're not prepared to take risks of that kind—to dare—not prepared to take so-called rebuffs; if you're not prepared to discipline your personality, the best thing is to go and play tiddlywinks and leave occultism entirely alone. If you can stand the pressures and the discipline and keep at it, then sooner or later the personality gives in and does what you tell it and not what it wants to do. Then you're truly progressing on the path.

In a group you'll often find people who don't seem to do anything at all; they get no results and yet they seem quite happy to be part of the group, contributing occasional work. You think, "What a useless kind of person!" Yet they may be an essential part of the group, because they are acting as a catalyst. In the same way that a catalyst causes changes in a chemical compound without itself being affected, they change things without themselves being changed in the process. There are people like that. They come into a group who have been getting nothing, nothing at all, and suddenly everything starts happening around the newcomer. These catalysts are very valuable people, and, curiously enough, they are more often than not redheaded.

In a group you have positive and negative elements, but this doesn't necessarily mean a man and a woman. You can get a woman who is far more positive than a man, and the magnetic currents work through her that way. You'll also find a man who is very much on the feminine side, and, in this case, the currents work in the reverse order. Put those two together and they work wonders. Very often a woman will take a positive part and make an excellent magus in the lodge; or on another occasion a man will provide the feminine element. Positive and negative elements can work very well in a lodge, but it tends to cause trouble when you get confused sexuality coming into the group and upsetting the whole polarity. Some people are working in reverse the whole time; and, because of that, if they are not watched, they can break up a group very, very quickly. And it's a nasty breakup. So whoever is in charge of a lodge has to work very carefully. They don't simply open the gates and let anybody come in. And that's where your outer court is useful; indeed, it's essential. The professed reason for the existence of the outer court is to give candidates instruction; but there is another reason: Newcomers can be watched to see how they are shaping up and what makes them tick before they're allowed into the active lodge where the work is being done and where powers are being wielded.

Questions from the Floor and Answers

Question: I remember reading Israel Regardie saying he thought before anyone went into magic or an occult group they should have some form of therapy or should be psychoanalyzed. Do you agree?

W.E.B.: Exactly, but not the ordinary psychoanalytical stuff. Psychologists vary so much among themselves. You have the Freudians; you have the Adlerians and the Watsonians. The Watsonians are the behaviorists; they say you're simply a chemical machine and everything you do is a conditioned reflex (like one of old Pavlov's dogs which salivated automatically whenever a bell rang because it associated the bell with dinner). The Watsonians dominate the American universities, but to my way of thinking—the occult way—William James is America's real psychologist of note.

Then there's C. G. Jung and I regard him as being the Darwin of modern psychology. There are now neo-Jungians who go a stage further than the master (and they should do so of course; you should never remain static or stereotyped). There are about fifty different schools of psychology, and, above all of them, is this inner school of psychology which belongs to the Mysteries and which is different in many respects. Jung is the nearest to this inner school. So, if you do feel you want to do something about self-analysis, Jungian psychology is the nearest in tune with the Mysteries.

Training the Personality:

THE GHOSTS
IN THE PARLOR

You will have noticed I've chosen some lovely titles—"The Rubbish in the Back Room," "The Ghosts in the Parlor"—that kind of thing. An old gnostic said, "The Soul of Man is a City." So you can regard yourself (your personality, that is) as being your house, your castle, or whatever you like. For the moment I'm regarding it as a house. We've been talking about getting rid of some of the rubbish in that back room. Now we come to the "Ghosts in the Parlor." What do I mean by that? Mostly we think of ghosts as cloaked in white sheets and peering round corners. Well, there are ghosts and ghosts. I would like to discuss the idea of reincarnation for a moment to show you the background of these "ghosts" as we call them.

We have a personality built up in this life on earth. We've built it up from scratch, but it's linked with the far distant past by the fact that the body we have comes to us from the animal ancestry of humanity. All events and happenings concerning it from immemorial times are stored in our personality in various ways. We carry within us the blueprint which determines whether our eyes are going to be blue, brown, or green, or whether we're going to be tall, short, or whatever. We also carry within us all kinds of recessive genes which link us back to the past, so that very often we suffer for our grandparents' faults. Thus, the sins of the fathers are visited upon the children. And this personality of ours has been brought about in that way. Why? In order that it may be developed as an instrument which we can use—"we" being the true self, the true I, the spirit self if you prefer to call it that. Behind that true self of ours is what is sometimes referred to as the "ground of the soul" or in Eastern terminology, "Atman," the Eternal.

You cannot divide the Eternal. Each one of us has one part of ourselves which is linked with the Infinite—which is, in fact, *part* of the Infinite. The other part of ourselves is linked with the ether in which we come and with that living planet we call the earth. So we are between the Heavenly Father and the Earthly Mother— again, you see, polarity comes into it. Not only the side polarity of the Tree of Life, but also the vertical polarity from Kether to Malkuth. The personality is adapted to the world and has certain jobs to do in the world. Because it's been built up in time and space, it is not immortal. (W. E. Butler will not live forever, not the personality W. E. Butler.) A personality is simply a mask which has been built up during the course of the years and which is an instrument in the hands of my higher self behind the scenes. That higher self contains within it many, many personalities from the past. Let's trace this personality through one cycle. I die and I pass into the astral world. There I begin to get rid of a lot of the impedimenta, a lot of the material within my self which is no longer of any use to me. I begin to rise to higher spheres; in other words, my personality changes and has a different outlook altogether. Like a man waking from a deep trance, it begins to know things, hear things, and understand things which it couldn't before, because it's coming closer to its source. This source is my true individuality behind the scenes. Finally, my personality is linked up with that individuality, and I'm back home, for the time being, with my true self.

If you like, you can imagine it through the symbolism of King Arthur's castle. A knight's been sent out to do a job; so off he goes into the wilderness and rescues a fair maiden or slays a dragon or gets mixed up in a lot of trouble. He returns to the castle, tired out and possibly damaged by the ordeals he's been through. He returns to the city from which he came. He's received back into the castle and another knight goes out into the wilderness. This knight has to pick up the job which the first knight has been doing. He has to redress the first knight's mistakes, put right those things he did wrong. So the second knight is linked with that knight (the personality) back in the castle and behind him all the time is the effect of that personality; there's a telepathic walkie-talkie between himself and the past personality. The essence of that past personality doesn't die; it is there in the higher self or the inner self. That being so, the next knight to go out for the fight has to come into the conditions the first and second knights have created; in other words, he has to pick up karma, the conditions created by the previous personalities. That's just a general view of reincarnation. There's lots more to it which I hope to come to later on.

On the way back to the true self, the old personality can communicate through a medium if he wishes; but all the time he's going upwards, he becomes less able to communicate because the average medium doesn't take the trouble to develop ethically to the extent that he or she should. Some mediums are quite definitely training for the spiritual path and trying to make of their mediumship something which will be of help to the world. Unfortunately, mediums get lumped together far too easily. There are those who will tell you about someone who has passed over or tell your fortune, that sort of thing. But that's only one element of it. There are many other mediums who are straight, upright, spiritually minded people who are really trying to advance. Through them you can obtain interesting insights into what happens to the personality in the higher stages of its career in the other world.

Finally, the personality is absorbed, as they say; but it isn't absorbed really any more than your childhood's consciousness is absorbed. As I explained earlier, it's still there and can be brought out by hypnosis. It sometimes happens that a former personality emerges from the higher self and becomes what the spiritualists call a "spirit guide," a guardian angel as it were, one of the old personalities pulled out from the city by the fact that the purity of the self is such that it can be done. When this happens, the other personalities remain where they are.

Then again, it's not always a beneficial personality that comes through. When this happens in an occult lodge, the members of the lodge become affected by the past—not only by karma, not only by what has happened in the past which is now causing trouble (perhaps physical, mental, or emotional problems, or struggles with the circumstances around them)—they are also affected by those old personalities and they affect them in a queer way. You may get up one morning feeling full of vim and vigor, determined to show the world what you can do, and, quite suddenly, you begin to feel a sort of power within you. So you tackle a particularly difficult job— thinking, "I can soon do this. There's nothing to it"—although ordinarily it's the kind of job you wouldn't dream of tackling at all. But you've had this terrific surge of power come through, and you think, "I'm being helped. I've been given power to do this."

But very often you're not being helped at all. What has happened is this: One of those old personalities has come in front of the spiritual sun within yourself and is casting its shadow over the present personality; you are now feeling as that old personality did. This personality may have been a king of a kingdom—powerful, autocratic, benevolent, or cruel—and the feeling and the power you get with it is the same feeling of the man as he lived then. It is that which has come through to overshadow you. When that happens, you can make the most appalling blunders because you're mistaking it for something else. So whenever you get a rush of power to the head, remember it may be nothing more than a reflex action of one of your old personalities coming through in this way, affecting your present consciousness. It happens more often than people realize.

There are many other things of that nature which comprise the body of what you might call esoteric psychology—elements which are neither Jungian nor Freudian but dependent upon the knowledge and the wisdom of the higher self. With this awareness, you find that you look at your personality in an entirely different way. You begin to notice factors which you hadn't seen before, not in ordinary life. But in the lodge they become intensified and I'm talking now of lodge training. When a person begins to get a rush of power in the way we've just spoken of, the heads of the lodge— if they know their business—will take extra precautions to squash it and to prevent it happening again, because it's no good to anyone. If the trouble isn't nipped in the bud, that person is going to upset the whole apple cart.

Those ghosts of the past can be the very devil because when they affect the personality, they bring with them contacts with a host of other things. It's as though they've come through muddy places; and when a ghost strikes a person's consciousness, it brings with it the power—and that particular power is to a certain extent contaminated. So whenever you start getting swell-headed—thinking you're all-wise, all-powerful, or even all-loving (even that can be overdone)—remember the Tree of Life and the balance of its teaching: Too much love is smotherliness (motherliness run riot); too much justice becomes cruelty and so on. You have to find a balance between the love and justice; otherwise, you get the Qliphoth,[1] the unbalanced force.

The problem is that when you start studying occultism and you feel these forces coming through, you invariably begin to think you are advancing. You often hear it said, "Look at the power I felt. It was terrific, nearly knocked me over." Yes, but that force coming through doesn't do you any good. It makes you feel you're somebody big, and self-aggrandizement creeps in and the people around you are affected by it too. You can cause a lot of trouble in your lodge by allowing that sort of thing to happen. Then again, the force can come through without your knowing, catching you unawares because it comes in a cyclic tide at the anniversaries of that old personality. When that happens, the forces seem to be linked more closely with the earth, thus more easily affecting your present personality.

These forces visit you on their anniversaries (as, of course, do ordinary ghosts). Very often the lady who was running away from the villain at Hampton Court or elsewhere is nothing more than a picture in the astral ether. But when the anniversary of that actual event comes round, it sometimes happens that the personality on the other side dreams about it (because you do dream on the other side), and that dream projects itself right down the line of astral images and shows itself as a ghost below. A real person isn't there at all; it's a personality simply dreaming back to the old times. It's a very fascinating aspect of esoteric psychology, because you can dream back to quite a lot of past events. It's the key to much pathology in occultism (so-called vampirisms and so-called lycanthropy, where people change into animals and that kind of thing). Somebody, somewhere, is dreaming back, and sometimes the dreaming has very serious consequences.

Another thing. When those ghosts materialize like that in your consciousness, if you don't watch out, they'll use you. While you think you're using them and the power they bring through, more often than not, the power is simply using you.

I'll give you an illustration. I was up in Scotland recently where the Scottish Nationalists were active. (You wouldn't believe the amount of animosity there is in Scotland among the nationalists. There's a real hatred of the English; it has to be experienced to be believed.) I was touring around with my wife and we came to Culloden. (Culloden, of course, was the scene of a battle. All the ideals and hopes of the Stuarts were lost there, and there's a very considerable atmosphere about the place.) We thought we'd go and take a look at a little cottage which was once the headquarters of the Battle of Culloden and still stands there intact today. It's a beautiful little place lit up with fluorescent lighting inside, nothing the least uncanny or dark about it. Then quite suddenly, as I went inside, I was knocked sideways. I began to see the atmosphere physically and it was foul, absolutely foul. There was a confused jumble of old forms—"shells" as we call them—forms of old Scottish personalities. Somebody had been evoking those shells. It can be done. There's a certain way of doing it, but it's a very nasty thing to do. But someone had evidently been having a go and those shells were alive and active. The evoker had put his own life-force into them. He had also brought through that power in the way that I was speaking of; it had affected him inasmuch as he had passed it through himself and charged those shells with it. I stayed about ten seconds. Then I said, "Goodnight," and left quickly because I wasn't going to attempt to deal with that particular atmosphere. There are certain things you rush into and others that you don't, and that was definitely one of the "don'ts." That's the kind of thing that can happen. You can easily charge a whole neighborhood if you allow those old ghosts from the past to bring through the terrific force which lies behind them. Although that power comes from the past, it can materially affect you in the present.

If anyone asks you to exorcise some thing or some place, don't rush in too quickly. Find out what kind of job you are up against. I suppose I've carried out five hundred or so exorcisms, but I've never taken them on lightheartedly. These powers—powers of darkness, if you like—are very real and they can affect you disastrously. It's all very well to say, "Now I know how to do this," and, in all the glory of your ignorance, you begin exorcising something that has a lot of teeth to it. And when you get bitten, you don't like it at all.

I've known cases of exorcisms backfiring. Here is one in particular: A man, a very good psychic and medium, used to go around with a Church of England clergyman. He and this clergyman went about together performing exorcisms. When the spirit or ghost came through the medium, the canon would chase him up, tell him he shouldn't be such a bad lad, and finally banish him by exorcism. All went well for quite a number of cases until one day they met up with a particular spirit that wouldn't be exorcised; instead, the spirit took control of the medium. Shortly after that, the poor old medium became involved in some very nasty immoral activities and there was the devil of a shout about it. Since then, that medium has done nothing; his social life is finished and he's on the scrap heap, so to speak. All because he took a chance where he shouldn't have.

Don't forget this: Good intentions pave the way to Hell; in themselves, they do not protect you from trouble. If your good intentions touch a twenty thousand volt line, you'll die. These forces on the inner planes are real forces. So, when it comes to exorcism—of either places, things, or people—be careful. There are safe ways of doing it, and you can learn them. You can practice under the advice and control of those who know the right way. But, don't—for Heaven's sake—do anything in the way of exorcism just for fun or because you think it ought to be done. It may "ought to be done," but are you the right person to do it? That's the point. Just because it's been brought to your attention doesn't mean you have to deal with it personally; it may have been brought to your attention so that you could pass it on to somebody who knows the right way to go about it. Always play for safety. The unseen realm contains all matter of things, all kind of beings. For instance, when you see an elemental[2] in its own natural habitat, it's the boss, not you. Unless you have permission of the elemental king concerned, you mustn't go knocking about with the elemental when he's at home. You try it and you'll be in for a considerable amount of trouble. Never, never overestimate your powers in occultism.

If you're going to be a real occultist and do work (not all the flimflam stuff, where if they did see a spirit, they'd go through the roof like a scalded cat), if you're really going to do the work, then you have to take precautions. You have to realize you're not the only pebble on the beach and you don't know everything. Out there are principalities and powers, Spirits of Wickedness in exalted places with the power to nip you if you don't watch out. Good intentions are no cover; good intentions plus knowledge are. But you have to know yourself as well as knowing the thing you're up against.

Now I want to deal with something else: The balance of the personality. That personality you are training for a definite job is always biased. You can overdo it with too much emotion, too much intellect, or too much sheer joy of living. Quite a lot of things you do in this life are out of balance, so you have to learn to balance. That is why we're applying qabalah, and we do so in a certain way. It's a very good practice with nothing that can be faulted. Take, for instance, Geburah—or Pachad, as it is sometimes known—which means fear and is the sphere of justice on the Tree. Now justice is impartial; it comes through the sword of Geburah. But you can overdo justice, and then it becomes injustice. You can make it too rigid, too harsh, and it becomes evil; it becomes qliphothic.

You can see it in your daily life. Wandering down the street one morning, you see the corporation bulldozer bringing down some slum dwellings. There goes the old chain up against the walls and they're down. What a pity, you think! A nice Victorian house destroyed! But why? Because they're going to build something good and better there. Geburah has done its job, a good job, and the opposite, Chesed, will begin to rebuild.

On the other hand you may see vandals getting into a house and destroying it—tearing out the light fittings, smashing the bath, and all the rest of it. They've got a vicious feeling against the place and are determined to wreck it. That's Geburah gone mad—out of balance—and that is evil. It's no use saying, "Oh well, the building was best out of the way." That may be, but it wasn't best out of the way by that method because the ground isn't cleared for rebuilding. You can have that in your own nature, that particular out-of-balance Geburah, and you may not even realize it. Say you have this overwhelming desire to cut somebody down to size—somebody with an innocent pride who is so proud of himself that he is beaming around, saying, "I've made a good job of that." And you might reply, "Yes, but why did you do it? Just because you wanted kudos?" You squash him flat and get a perverse feeling of pleasure in doing so. And that's evil. You're acting as a qliphothic agent then. So whenever you feel like cutting another down to size, just make sure it isn't you that's out of balance, using Geburah in an out-of-balance way. It is the same with all the other sephiroth on the Tree of Life; they all have their unbalanced aspect. In astrology, we call it the malefic aspect.

If you want equilibrium, which is the basis of all magical work, you have to balance the forces within you. It's so easy to let ourselves go one way or the other, swing with the pendulum. But we have to resist that if we are to achieve anything at all. We have to balance all the side paths in favor of the middle path, which is the only true path. Not until we've balanced the side pillars can we take the path of the arrow straight through to Kether, to completion. It's most important because then you get away from the idea of sin and think in terms of balancing. That may sound peculiar, but there is sin and sin—there's evil and evil.

One form of evil is the thrust block of the universe, the resistance of matter to spirit. That is evil, but it's a primal evil which is good because it serves the divine purpose. Try skating on a frictionless piece of ice and you won't get very far; try walking on a frictionless surface and you'll find you fall down before you've taken two or three steps. There must be friction, something to give you a thrust. So the thrust block of the universe is referred to as "negative evil." It means this: You don't have to make things unduly rough to thrust off; but you do have to have some resistance, and that resistance is implicit in the universe. It is the testing element in the universe, and Satan is the tester. Your passage on earth is disputed, and the ones who embody that principle are the satans who are tempting and testing you.

In the Lord's Prayer there is a passage "Lead us not into temptation"; and the spiritualists along with many others get all bothered about that. They ask, "How can they say that of God? That He could lead people into temptation?" But St. James says quite clearly, "Let no man say, when he is tempted, 'I am tempted of God,' for God cannot be tempted with evil; neither tempteth He any man. Every man is tempted when he is drawn away of his own lust."[3] St. James didn't mince his words. Nevertheless, there is a certain amount of truth in the passage. Translation is the trouble; translation always fogs things up. Scholars are now saying that the true translation of this passage is: "Bring us not to the test." In other words, "Until I'm ready, please don't throw me in at the deep end." Simply that: "Leave me not alone when I'm in temptation."

Then there's another kind of evil. We have negative evil and we have negative-negative evil; and that is not a question of inertia, but more of quicksand. There are certain forms of existence which exist both in the far depths of the universe and in the far depths of ourselves which are the qliphothic equivalents to the bogs of Ireland. Once you're in them, you're quickly overwhelmed and sucked down. It often occurs with people who have gone through a very traumatic experience, and they're left wondering if life is worth the candle. They get into Bunyan's "slough of despond." (That's a very good name for it. Bunyan's book[4] is a Westernized form of initiation; every one of its characters can be fitted into the story of initiation. Perhaps Bunyan wrote about more than he realized.) This slough of despond engulfs you; and if you get into that evil, you not only go right out (a lot of people commit suicide at that phase); you also affect others around you in a regrettable way. So when you get that feeling of being absolutely trapped, then it's the time to start moving because you're not only at risk yourself; you're putting others at risk, too. You're acting as a kind of fever carrier, like a typhoid carrier. Wherever you go, you carry that atmosphere with you and it infects other people. Remember that and don't let it get started because, like a lot of other things, once it does, it takes control. But you can stop it before it gets very far by diverting the mind altogether and doing something different, absolutely opposite. Then you begin to swing the pendulum the other way.

Still another form of evil is positive evil. Many people say that evil is the absence of good. That's a great phrase among the "new thought" people: "There isn't such a thing as real evil. It's the ab-

sence of good," they say. In one sense they are quite correct. It is
the absence of good in the same way that darkness is the absence of
light. But positive evil, on the other hand, is being worked upon
by a living consciousness. It's no longer the personal evil of the
thrust block of the universe. It is the resistance to the will of the
Creator, to the will of the Logos, and that resistance is a positive
resistance. It makes for sadism; it makes for vivisection and cruelty.
It makes for the Holy Inquisition, Hitler and the gas ovens, and all
the rest of the foulness which humanity has displayed during its
course upon the earth. It has been with us since the beginning of
mankind. The Babylonians used to build high towers of loose sand,
put their victims on top, and watch them slowly sink into the sand.
It was the Inquisition that drew people from the villages to watch
others being burned alive. That spirit is not yet dead by any manner
of means. You can still have a witch hunt. Occultists in some parts
of the world still receive this kind of treatment. It was only in
eighteen hundred and something that the last person was burned
alive for witchcraft; that was in Ireland, not in some far Patagonian
state. The burning was carried out by the mob, the mob mind
getting loose again. That is positive evil, and it exists. You can close
your eyes and say, "Oh well, all these people are misguided and
misdirected. It isn't really their fault; it's their upbringing and environment," but you could be very wide of the mark. There is real
positive evil in the world; and, as an occultist, you'll find part of
your work is putting that kind of thing right by balancing the forces.
And the Tree of Life is one of the instruments we use.

I've digressed into this subject because it is important that we
shouldn't minimize evil when we meet it. At the same time, we
shouldn't try to make too much of it; we shouldn't try to make it
something terrible. "Satan trembles when he sees the weakest saint
upon his knees." That's a hymn I've heard sung on several occasions and it's true enough: Satan, the great fallen angel, lord of the
fallen hosts. When the weakest saint (by saint, the hymnist meant a
fellow Christian) gets on his knees, Satan goes. In other words, you
have power behind you against all that sort of thing. The power of
the Divine in Whom you live and move and have your being and
of Whom you are a part. So you need never worry about the pow-

ers of darkness. All the same, don't get into positions where they are liable to bite you. If they do, see to it that you bite back, that you conquer the thing.

Now, all this work results in what you might call quite a nice personality. You've built yourself up, trained yourself, and you've become, more or less, an "adeptus minor." Lovely title that! After slogging your way through all the grades, you've finally made it to adeptus minor. Wonderful! Dion Fortune presents a good picture of the minor adept in her books *Moon Magic* and *The Sea Priestess.*[5] When you are a minor adept you can speak the words of power and something will happen when you do (It's fantastic. You're within an ace of moving the whole works). When you get to that point and you are sure you have achieved it, that's the moment you're most liable to fall. "Let him that thinketh he standeth take heed lest he fall."[6] You've got to be standing, but you have to be standing in another strength. This means you have to let go of all that lovely personality—that adeptus minor you've built up with all the knowledge, all the wisdom, all the know-how. You have to give it up completely.

St. Paul says, "Though I speak with the tongues of men and of angels, and have not charity, I am become as sounding brass or a tinkling cymbal. And though I have the gift of prophesy, and understand all mysteries, and all knowledge; and though I have all faith, so that I could remove mountains, and have not charity, I am nothing."[7] And by charity, of course, St. Paul means love.

Now love is not emotion. It is an attitude of the mind and the spirit which can be as cold as ice for the benefit of the loved one. You wouldn't want to be operated on by a surgeon with a blunt scalpel, would you? Yet many people think of love in that way; they're emotionally, not mentally, affected. They say they love a person because they feel emotion. But that's not love; it's simply power going out, emotional power going out from them. It isn't love. It may be selfish power; it may be smother love. It depends entirely upon how our love ideal is balanced.

In any case, when we have our perfect personality, our adeptus minor, we move on to another step—to the superpersonality. We've really made something now. We are the boss of the group, a king in our own right. We're an adeptus major. We've come to the Abyss.

We've come to that line across the Tree of Life which says, "Here's a different thing altogether. This is not the personality; this is not your individuality any longer; this is something deeper still." You come to the Abyss and either you succeed or fail; there's no half measure. If you fail, then all that lovely personality you've built has been thrown away.

Your personality has been altered just like that lovely caterpillar and its cocoon is lost completely as the butterfly emerges. So when you come to the Abyss, all that personality you've built with such care is altered. It's changed just as the Bible says it will be changed. Then, on the other side, you are reborn as the child, the "Babe of the Abyss," as it is called. This consciousness, compared with the old consciousness, is a babe because it is learning something entirely new. It is a consciousness which is based upon the old personality; it carries all the old personality's good points with it, everything that was real in it. But it's bringing it now into an initiation, into a life so great, so wonderful, that everything that went before—all the heavens of the inner world—mean nothing to it at all. This consciousness stands in the divine realm—in the presence of the gods, as the old Egyptian ritual has it—and it sees face to face the Eternal Spirit of Whom it is a part. That is the perfection of man, the perfection of the personality. He's home, the home for which he's been longing all the time. But there's many a weary life, many a weary period of years, before we ever get anywhere near that. Still, there is an eternal home, far beyond anything our minds can conceive.

> *My soul, there is a country*
> *Far beyond the stars,*
> *Where stands a winged sentry*
> *All skilfull in the wars;* [8]

So says that great mystical poet, Henry Vaughan.

There is true peace, true happiness; everything is there in the Eternal. That is the goal of the Mystic, too, that he should be united with that One Eternal Life behind all other things, the nirvana of the Buddhists. It is known as "the blown-out state." Like a candle being blown out, the consciousness is blown out. That doesn't mean to say that everything is lost; the consciousness is blown out because the sun has arrived; the candle is no longer needed; it has been used and has made conditions by which the sun can shine. Now the candle is out, and the Sun of the Eternal shines through that being who is now a master in nirvana. That's the destiny of every one of us, every single one of us. We are children of earth, but we are also from the starry heavens.

In the occult lodges, we work on our personalities and make them as good as we possibly can, again and again and again. Then the *"Flyer will descend into the Sea."* The flyer is our personality imaged as a bird. It descends into the sea of the unconscious. There, in the unconscious, it is taken apart and reconstituted—like the phoenix which rose from its own ashes and returned all glorious to life again. Again and again the flyer will descend into the sea, and every time that happens, wider and wider will our consciousness grow—until, finally, we attain God consciousness, cosmic consciousness (call it what you will). Even in this life, we may sometimes experience it. I know of people who have had flashes of cosmic consciousness; but, as a general rule, they keep their mouths shut about it. There's a book on the subject by Dr. Bucke[9] dealing with some of the cases where people have had this flash of consciousness. This experience will come to every one of us in time if we're not in too much of a hurry. But, if we try to force it, to get there before we are ready, we're like a puppy with its eyes still closed. Open its eyes forcibly before they're ready to open naturally, and you can ruin its eyesight. And, if we try to go too fast, we sometimes blind ourselves to spiritual realities. So the motto is "Make haste slowly."

Questions from the Floor and Answers

Question: There's just one point I didn't quite understand. You started off by talking about exorcism and saying you could get your fingers burned quite severely. Later on you said that even a minor saint could make Satan tremble, if that saint knelt in prayer.

W.E.B.: You can't connect the two? Well, look at it this way: There is a divine foolishness which can get you through some remarkable scrapes, but there is also an earthly foolishness which can land you in trouble. Again, it's the question of the personality. The saint is praying to a higher being and he is getting out of the way and letting that higher being work through him. But, when you try doing it with, or through, your own strength ("I'm the exorcist in the midst of the exorcism. I command you to depart from this person, or this place, or whatever"), it very often happens that the one at the other end, the one you're trying to exorcise, says, "And who are you to command?" Then it bites you.

Remember in the New Testament some of the disciples went out to perform a little exorcism. They came back and said to the Lord, "Even the Spirits are subject to us in Thy Name."[10] But there were the seven sons of Sceva the Jew, who thought, "If these Galileans can do this trick, then so can we." Thus, they went forth to try their hands at exorcism. They took hold of a person possessed of an evil spirit and tried to exorcise it. But the spirit turned on them and said, "Jesus I know, and Paul I know; but who are ye?" Then the evil spirit attacked the sons of Sceva and treated them violently until they fled the house, naked and wounded.[11] So you see, you can attempt things in your own pride and open the door to those forces of evil. Never go into exorcism with the idea that I will do this, because you darn well won't, not in your own strength you won't. But it, the thing you want to exorcise, might do something, something you won't like!

Question: What you're saying then is that in exorcism you call upon another power to work through you?

W.E.B.: Exactly, you never do it in your own strength. Your power is utilized as a kind of focus or lever to do the work, but the hand on the lever is not yours. I've had practical experience of that, believe me. I've come unstuck at odd times. If anyone tells you they've never come unstuck, don't believe them because in occultism we all come unstuck frequently. We're bound to, human nature being what it is.

Question: You said at the start that the rush of power going to the head can be nothing more than an old personality coming through. How do you tell the difference, whether it's an old personality coming through or something else you've made contact with?

W.E.B.: There's a big difference. I can't say any more than this. How can you tell the difference between the taste of an orange and the taste of a plum? There's a difference, but can you describe that difference? Only by taste, possibly that one appears more sour than the other. Then you have subjective terms, "taste, sourness, my taste, your taste," and so on. You see you have to qualify it by other things. All I can add is this: Once you've experienced that power, you won't mistake it.

> *Whoso has felt the Spirit of the Highest*
> *Cannot confound nor doubt Him nor deny:*
> *Yea with one voice, O world, tho' thou deniest,*
> *Stand thou on that side, for on this am I.*[12]

And that's it. When that power hits you, you'll recognize it. You'll know without any doubt. I think it is in one of the lessons of the B.O.T.A. (Builders of the Adytum). It is stressed that you have to experience that power to be able to understand it. You won't get it by mental thinking.

Training the Personality:

THE ACTORS
IN THE LOUNGE

I would now like to talk to you about the psychological side of things. You will recall we mentioned the idea that there is an esoteric psychology which is more effective than the ordinary headshrinker's variety and depends upon the arcane tradition which stands behind all orders.

Back in 1924 when I first came in touch with Dion Fortune, she was trying to evolve this system of esoteric psychology for the benefit of her students. It soon became evident that she was being helped by the people on the inner planes. They gave her a valuable outline for this particular work; and, during the early days of the Inner light, she evolved that knowledge into quite a workable scheme. Those students who came under it had reason to thank Providence for the opportunity because it helped them to understand themselves ("Man, Know Thyself," as we are so often adjured to do). There's an interesting, philosophical poem by Alexander Pope that goes:

> *Know then thyself, presume not God to scan,*
> *The proper study of mankind is man.*
> *Placed on this isthmus of a middle state,*
> *A being darkly wise, and rudely great:*
> *With too much knowledge for the sceptic side,*
> *With too much weakness for the stoic's pride,*
> *He hangs between; in doubt to act or rest;*
> *In doubt to deem himself a god, or beast;*
> *In doubt his mind or body to prefer;*

> *Born to die, and reas'ning but to err;*
> *Alike in ignorance, his reason such,*
> *Whether he thinks too little or too much;*
> *Chaos of thought and passion, all confused;*
> *Still by himself abused, or disabused;*
> *Created half to rise, and half to fall;*
> *Great lord of all things, yet a prey to all;*
> *Sole judge of truth, in endless error hurled;*
> *The glory, jest, and riddle of the world!*

That comes from Pope's *An Essay on Man*[1] and is well worth your study if you come across it.

If we know ourselves, we know our weaknesses and our strengths. We begin to see who we really are and what we are and exactly what our potential is. Then we don't do foolish things, like attempting something way beyond our present capabilities. We keep within our limits. And there's a lot to be said for keeping within one's limits. Of course there will always be times when we step beyond those limits, but not inadvertently and not without forethought because that spells trouble.

If you are coming into occultism with serious intentions—that is to say, you're a worker as well as a talker—then you have to realize there are times when you don't forge ahead and there are times when you do. It so often depends upon the inner tides which flow through you, tides of all kinds which we will come to presently.

First, we must realize that we are all more or less asleep, not really awake at all. We've evolved over the years a secondary personality, a mask which we place in front of ourselves to prevent others seeing us as we really are. We would prefer them to see us as we think they ought to see us. For example, when someone's coming to tea or coming to dine with you, what happens? You spruce yourself up; whereas, if it were just the family you were eating with, you wouldn't bother about all that sprucing. But, when it's important for you to present a certain face to someone, then you spruce up. We all do that. It's a common trait of humanity to adjust our personalities to please or interest the people we meet. Think

about it and you'll realize you do just that. Whomever you're talking to, you try to impress them with your own personality, your
own self. When you're talking to yet another person, you find you
adopt a different variety of tactics; a different side of your nature
comes out, a different aspect of your personality. But, when pre-
senting your best face (or mask) to your enemies, you find they
draw out from you a certain automatic reaction. You can't help it,
it's involuntary, something you haven't yet learned to control. They
bring out either the worst in you or the best in you. You've no
doubt heard people say, "Old So-and-so brings out the worst in
me." It's an effective action upon one personality by another personality. These clashes of personalities are not merely because we
do not like the look of the other's face or the sound of their voice
or we don't like something they've said. There is underneath a
steady, telepathic pressure getting at us.

Don't underestimate telepathy. We live in a sea of it; we are
surrounded by it. All the time our thoughts are going out to other
people and other people's thoughts are coming in to us. They con-
stitute a real range of experience of which we haven't the slightest
conception because it's all going on below the surface of consciousness.

The fact that it happens below the level of consciousness doesn't
mean we are not affected by it. We are, and very much so. When
talking about another person, people sometimes say, "I won't say
anything about him, but I can think what I like." I've said it myself,
but it's wrong. You can't think what you like— or rather you can,
but you take the consequences of what you think, because we are
all linked together in this peculiar telepathic way. When you think,
you send out thought forms. Some people send out lovely ones and
others not so lovely. If you're clairvoyant, you can sometimes see
them— nasty little things or beautiful little things, as the case may
be. In any case, we are continually sending out this stream of thought.
We can't help ourselves. We are man (*manas*, the thinker) and so
we must always be sending out these waves of thought. We're
natural radio sets, continually transmitting.

Suppose we see someone, say a lady who hasn't a very whole-
some reputation. We're watching her from across the street; we

mustn't say anything about her—oh no, that would be unchari-
table—but we can think what we like. And so we do. We think
what we like, and out goes an ugly little thought form with considerable power because it has emotion behind it, and it pitches on
that lady's aura. Now, that particular lady may have been fighting
temptation and fighting it hard. She may have been teetering on a
razor edge of giving in to a particular impulse that wasn't good and
just managing to resist it. She's like someone crossing a chasm on a
narrow bridge. Along comes your nasty little thought form hitting
her when she's off balance, and she falls for the temptation she has
been trying so hard to resist. It has nothing to do with you? But it
does. When the day comes that hearts are weighed and records
examined, yours will be the major responsibility for that woman's
transgression. Without your interference, she may have come to
the right decision, but you—with your nasty little thought form—
knocked her sideways onto the wrong path.

When you are an occultist and begin to think with the trained
mind of an occultist, your thinking can be deadly. Because you are
trained, you can produce thought forms which are so real and so
vivid that under certain conditions they can actually materialize
and be seen with the physical eye. I've done it so I know. We
rarely think without infusing our thoughts with emotion. The only
time we don't is when we're working at mathematics; and, even
then, it's possible when your sums won't come right that you get
peeved about it. But thinking about ordinary things, thinking about
people, you can put a considerable amount of emotion into what
you're thinking. So don't forget: As a trained occultist you are responsible for your thoughts in a way that an untrained person is
not, simply because you have the power to make these vivid and
strong thought forms. They can even affect places and buildings.
I've been to places where an infestation of unpleasant thought forms
has been built up by someone with an elementary knowledge of
thought power, and that atmosphere was nasty, very nasty indeed.
And where it has been accompanied by pain, it becomes doubly
powerful. That is why places which have been subjected to the
thoughts of people who have endured great pain and suffering—
Buchenwald, for instance—carry a terrific charge and power of
emotional cruelty and feeling.

Now hypnosis is something which has long been regarded with a kind of superstitious awe; yet we are all in a state of hypnosis. We've built up our personality to follow a certain line of thinking and feeling and we've locked ourselves into that. That's a form of hypnosis. We're sleepwalking to some extent. We do things automatically (like that London crowd we were talking about), not thinking about what we are doing—just going ahead blindly with the vague idea we have to be at the office at a certain time, not really doing anything constructive, simply letting a current of thought go through our minds. That's what the majority of people do.

It isn't very difficult to be hypnotized. You can hypnotize yourself. In fact, you have to under certain conditions. Get rid of the idea that there's mystery regarding hypnotism, that you can be dominated by somebody else. The only person who can dominate you is you. If you allow yourself to think that you can be dominated, then of course you can be. It's tantamount to giving the key of the castle to the hypnotist or the chap concerned and saying, "Here you are; here's the key. Come right in and help yourself." So of course he comes in. But, if you keep the key in your own hands, nobody can hypnotize you against your will or make you do anything that is alien to your nature. We know there are people who are sometimes weak and foolish enough to let themselves be hypnotized against their wills; but that's because, basically, they've already hypnotized themselves into believing that the other person can influence them. That's the point. But deep down each of us knows that no other person can affect us against our will—they may try, and trying to do such a thing is black magic. If you try influencing someone subliminally to lend you money, you're indulging in black magic. It may not sound like very much, but it's black magic all the same. For instance, this subliminal advertising we hear about, that's a form of black magic. You can have little blackbirds as well as big blackbirds, and enough little blackbirds make up quite a weight. And so it is with those thoughts when we try to dominate somebody else. The moment we start that, we're on the wrong path and heading for real trouble.

All those advertisements which tell you how you can acquire the power to make friends and influence others are wrong, absolutely wrong. You must not do that. You can try to improve yourself so that you give a favorable image to people around you. You can work to improve yourself so that you give something of value in return for that which Providence, or karma, or whatever, gives to you. That's fair enough.

Say you want something badly, another house perhaps. You visualize it vividly, distinctly (how many rooms it has, which way it faces, the arrangements of the rooms, perhaps with a little bit of land). You build it up as firmly and as clearly as you can. That is practical magic. You create this "composition of place," as it is called in magic. You do it the same way when you're working ceremonial magic. But you must make it clear and distinct in your mind and you say: "This is what I desire. This is what I feel would be best for me, and I ask positively." Ask (demand if you like!) "that it shall come to me, if it be the will of God." Always that proviso, "if it be the will of God." I've seen scores of cases where people have worked that kind of magic and the thing they wanted has materialized. It was the will of God; they worked with that will and they got what they wanted. But they wouldn't have succeeded if they hadn't first visualized clearly what it was they really wanted. They were exercising some of the God power within them, be-cause—and always remember this—our thought is the power of the God within.

If you really want something badly, you can do the same thing: Visualize it clearly and distinctly as to color, as to form, as to ap-pearance, as to everything; visualize it all as vividly as your imagina-tion can make it. If you have artistic leanings, make a sketch and paint it and make it definite in your mind so that you have a true picture. Then say: "If this is the will of the Divine Life, if this is possible, then I ask for it positively." Do it in the same way as a child might ask of its father, "Father, give me so-and-so if it will be good for me." Now the moment you say that, it sounds a bit pious; but it isn't really. It's the law at work. I've seen it work many times. When people have tried this particular bit of magic without that proviso at the end, they've got what they wanted and it's come unstuck in their hands. Oh, yes! Their will, their power, their thought power was so great, they had built a thought form and it had attracted to them the very thing they wanted. But it came at the wrong time and they couldn't use it—or, as in some cases, it overwhelmed them; and they couldn't manage it. It was worse for them at the end than it was in the beginning. So you always ask for something subject to the will. I've heard it many times in the East, "If it be the will of Allah, then it will be so." And you accept that. But you don't say that, and hope you've caught the Old Man when He's not looking your way and didn't understand properly and will grant it nevertheless. You don't try to get round the side of God with that little trick. Some do, you know. They seem to think they can catch God off guard, as it were. But you can't. God is not mocked. If you try it, you will only be sorry for it later on.

Long ago, I made a fool of myself. I tried to force Providence to do that which I wanted. Providence did, but I wasn't looking out for it; and the flood came when my back was turned. Before I could make use of it, I was overwhelmed by it. It took me quite a long time before I sorted myself out again. There are times when, if you are not careful, you catch a cold in occultism. I've caught a few in my time. Still, I must be pretty tough because I've managed to come through this far.

Reverting to the subject of hypnotism: On one occasion I hypnotized a person and, taking an ordinary pencil, I said to this fellow, "With your permission I'm going to try an experiment. I'm going to mark your arm by using a redhot needle so it will burn your arm. However, you won't feel anything at all; you won't feel a single moment of pain or discomfort. But I would like to try this demonstration while you are in this hypnotic condition. Have I your permission to do so?"

"Yes," the man said, "just so long as I don't feel any pain. Go ahead!" So, with an ordinary pencil, I drew a small triangle on his arm. Within the minute, where I had drawn that line, up came a triangular burn. There was fluid beneath the skin and true blisters; both were immediately produced by the subconscious mind to separate the two layers of skin and so prevent the underskin from being damaged. That particular automatic mechanism went into action straight away. That is the tremendous power which hypnotism has of altering your state of consciousness.

Altered states of consciousness are regarded nowadays as being something occult. But that's not so. You can alter your state of consciousness in many ways. You can drink a pint of beer, for instance. It depends entirely on how you are adjusted—that is, what your tolerance to alcohol is—as to how exactly your consciousness will be altered. My own tolerance is very low and half a pint of beer is sufficient. Any more, and I'm in trouble. We all have that innate level, and changing consciousness can be a tricky matter—more so if you use psychedelic drugs. I want to touch upon those because I am, perhaps, a bit fanatical about them. But I've seen the aftereffects of drug taking. I've seen the complete breakdown of a personality. I've seen a bright, intelligent youth, who could have been something in the world and a help to others, become a neurotic, whimpering wreck, frightened of his own shadow, all because of psychedelic drugs. Oh, yes, they will open up the gates of perception, but getting those gates closed again is a different matter. You step into the unknown of the unconscious; you don't know what's waiting for you. Nothing's been organized; there's been no training. Whatever comes up, you see it in all its glory—or in all its hideousness. Not only do we have within us the beautiful drawing room, the lounge and bedrooms, we also have the cellar and the sewers. Each one of us has a pretty considerable sewer down below with things which belong to the past of human evolution—the "dog-faced demons" as they are called in magic. We possess a lovely crew of those down below; and, if we go wandering into the unconscious, we are just as likely to meet up with them; they are our pals—the pals we made in the past—and they are linked to us by the very fact that we are their creator.

I wouldn't want anybody to think there is anything dignified about the "Dweller on the Threshold." People tend to glamorize it, saying the dweller on the threshold is all past karma coming up. But there are two dwellers, the greater and the lesser. Let's take a look at the lesser.

To face the dweller on the threshold means this: With your normal consciousness you come into a condition that makes you acutely aware. That sewage down below, that collection of psychic filth which we've collected and stored away very carefully is down there in the sewer. It's there and it's a part of us. We cannot tell ourselves, "Oh I don't possess anything like that. I never think about that sort of thing." Underneath we do, and sometimes it comes to the top. For instance, we've all heard about the parson's wife, who under anesthetic, gave voice to sentiments and opinions that were quite definitely unparsonly. It can happen in hypnosis. When you get this dweller on the threshold rearing its ugly head, then you get something nasty. So you don't want to go fooling around with amateur hypnosis. Don't touch a person and say, "Look, you can't use your hand now. It's too heavy for you; you can't even lift it. Try it, have a go." The subject tries and finds he can't. He thinks that it's true, that he can't move it. And he's frightened. That's the first onslaught on the castle. You've made him give you the key. And, if you start doing that, you're going to sup sorrow with a longhandled spoon before you're much older.

So, when you're thinking of changing consciousness, avoid the psychedelic drugs because they pitch you into a condition where you don't know where or what you are. You may strike beautiful scenes (some do, we know). These are the least destructive drug experiences. Nevertheless they are not good for this reason: You may see this lovely scene in your consciousness, but the drug also affects the chemical rhythms in your physical body. And upon those rhythms depend how closely you are in touch with the physical plane, how much you can control your body. Any psychedelic drug will leave harmful effects in the body. So steer clear of them! I can't say that too often.

You can try to raise your consciousness in order to become psychic or to look in on the inner planes (of course you have the power to do this). I want to talk about the pituitary gland. Serotonin is a rare chemical which the pituitary body secretes in very small quantities. When serotonin goes into the bloodstream, it has the effect upon the consciousness of inducing psychic vision. All your thinking, as far as your brain is concerned, is in chemical terms. You think, but it is the chemical changes in the brain which help you to think in the body. You have a very wonderful chemical system up there. So the natural clairvoyant opening up his or her clairvoyant powers actually starts the secretion of serotonin in the pituitary body, and that begins to open up the psychic centers. Now, if you take that same drug in a minute quantity, you'll induce psychic visions in yourself—even though you don't arouse the pituitary body. It has been done and is being done. I think it is dangerous myself because when you start poking your finger into the works like that, you don't know what the outcome may be. But that's how it works. It's a purely chemical process that goes on in the brain and in the pituitary center. The pituitary body is also the center of the third eye so you can see how the two connect.

Dion Fortune used to say that shifting the consciousness is the key to all occult training. It's quite true ("Fantasy is the ass that carries the ark."). She also maintained that in willed disintegration and reintegration is the secret of the Mysteries. When you read her books, have an eye out for odd sentences because she used to drop them in like raisins in a plum pudding. And those sentences have a tremendous amount of meaning in them. She's giving you a key or two; she camouflages it beautifully; but it's there if you look for it. For instance, in *Moon Magic* she gives a description of astral travelling which is a valid way of inducing astral projection. But, if you read the book merely as a piece of occult fiction, you may not consciously realize this. Many occult writers do it—camouflage the teaching, put a blind up, as we say—and there are lots of blinds in occult literature. Well, some of it is literature; and some of it isn't, unfortunately.

Changing consciousness by wines, liquor, or drugs is always a risky business. You never leave the personality just as it was before. We know that alcoholism is becoming one of the major diseases of the Western world. We've become so used to regarding alcohol as being a light refreshment or a social drink but, for many people who are sensitive, it becomes a dangerous drug. So we have Alcoholics Anonymous trying to put things straight. As you know, they tell you that you have to abstain totally; you take just one drink and you are back where you started—just that one drink and your whole body chemistry alters. So, if you do drink, temperance is the word; but temperance doesn't necessarily mean doing without. Moderation is the answer. You can drink and get away with it just so long as you know exactly where your tolerance lies and you stay within that limit.

Some people find that they are so sensitive that alcohol affects them drastically and that even half a pint is too much. Any person who is an occultist and tries to pressure another into drinking over his limit is committing black magic because he's mucking about with that person's mind and he ought to know better. Whatever you may hear or read to the contrary, you are responsible for your brother in a very real way and you must never drive him to exceed his tolerance level. Another person may be able to drink half a gallon and it doesn't make any difference. But, if you try to influence someone to drink when they really don't want to or when their capacity is very low, then you are committing a crime against that personality. And, sooner or later, you'll pay for it.

How, then, are we going to alter consciousness? We can do it by altering that chemical composition within ourselves by means of the power of thought, thereby influencing the pituitary gland to manufacture serotonin. Now, that autotrance into which you enter is a peculiar state of consciousness which gives you mastery over many of your inner faculties and inner powers. So, when you first start working with it, you must take it slow and steady, very slow and steady. Spectacular things, like raising blisters, are not advised. You go along with easy experiments, getting your consciousness accustomed to the idea that it can be altered by your thinking.

When you begin to do that, you find you are building yourself a new personality, not the same mask that you built up and which you regarded so fondly. You find another personality building up inside, something quite different. We call it the "magical personality." You train yourself to develop that magical personality. Let's take an example. You are going to raise the spirit of Mars, so you go into your magic circle and you have around you all the things which remind you of your primary intention. You have red drapes, red vestments, a sulphur incense in your thurible—a really good choking smell of Mars. You wield an iron wand. In fact, everything about you, everything you use, is associated with Mars in your mind. In this way you begin to feel yourself coming into contact with the Martian force. Wearing your red vestment, you conjure Mars; and, as you do this, your personality begins to take the shape of the Martian image. You are verily the controller of Mars. You feel, "I have the power; it's in me." And you feel you've only got to raise your hand and a shaft of red light will dart across the room and hit the ceiling. You feel like that because the magical personality has become very powerful; and, when you feel like that, and not until then, can you work the Martian ritual as it should be worked and get results.

I know a couple, man and wife, who worked the ritual in their little lodge, just the two of them. The man who was naturally a bit on the Martian side thought he really had the power. And quite suddenly there was a flash and a fiery flame ran right across the altar cloth searing it in two. He had the power all right, but he let it get out of control.

When Elisha called down fire from heaven at the time when he was fighting the priests of Baal, he was possibly doing the same thing. Because he felt that with the power of Jehovah he was able to control the fire, he brought the fire down.[2]

You possess powers within you which are beyond all ordinary thought, and you can realize them in your magical personality. I don't advise you to play around with it though. But, if you set out to build up a magical personality (I've gone deeply into this in one of my books,[3] disclosing how it can be done, and there are plenty of other people who have said the same thing in different ways), remember, you can only build up your magical personality legitimately for this one reason: in order that it may be an extra instrument in your service to God and mankind. If I develop my magical personality just to hear someone say—"What a wonderful magician Mr. Butler is. I saw fire coming out of his ears"—that's all wrong. If I had done something along those lines, it wouldn't prove what a wonderful magician I am; it would simply prove what a damn fool I am. I've got dynamite, but instead of using it to excavate a rock and obtain the precious metal, I've been playing around and showing off about it. One of the biggest dangers for occultists is when they start showing off what they know and what they can do.

Some people dabble with divination, play around with *The I Ching*[4] and the tarot cards. They become very skillful in the art; and if they would do it seriously and carry it on to what I call the "upper octaves," they would get some wonderful results. But, no, they have to demonstrate what wonderful technique they have. Eventually they drift into vulgar fortune-telling and the real intuitive knowledge that had been coming through by meditating on the cards is lost. Read Paul Foster Case's book on the tarot.[5] It will give you more insight on how to use the tarot than any number of books which tell you how to use the cards for fortune-telling.

So you've been building up your magical personality. It's there within your grasp. All you have to do to bring it into action is to change your consciousness; immediately you are the magician in the midst of magic and, by doing your stuff, you've turned on the switch and the power is there. Now there's all the difference in the world between doing this in a perfunctory sort of way—getting all hot and bothered about it and dashing round the circle getting nowhere—and the reality. The trained magician doesn't get hot and bothered and start waving his hands about, as I've seen some do. But calmly with his trained will, he says, "This working we are about to perform shall be on the inner planes," and it is. He has stated the intention clearly and precisely. His will is working on the inner planes as it should work, without fuss and without bother.

The same thing happens in hypnosis. When the inner will, quietly and without fuss, says "This pain shall go" or "This swelling shall subside," it works. But, if you try all manner of vigorous methods in an attempt to get rid of that pain or that swelling, it just won't work. It is the calm inner will of the magical personality which produces results. When you have done that, you've changed consciousness.

Because you have probably heard through the occult network that in some lodges psychedelic drugs have been used occasionally, I had better say something about that. They have been used, yes, and I repeat, occasionally. But they have been used in a special way and when used that way, you cannot hurt yourself. We've all heard of homeopathy. Homeopathy consists in taking a certain drug which will produce the same effect in a human being as the disease he is suffering from. Say a person has measles with a lot of spots and a fever. A drug which will produce the same results on a person in good health is held to be the remedy for that particular disease. The homeopathic doctor takes the remedy and puts one drop of the remedy in a jar of water. He shakes it and shakes it and shakes it again and again and again. Then, into yet another jar of water, he puts one drop of the mixture he's just shaken. This same process can go on for thirty or forty operations until it is well and truly diluted. Each mixture is called a potency. Chemical analysis can hardly tell if there's anything in the water, and yet the homeopathic doctor gives the patient a little sugar pill containing an infinitesimal part of the original remedy; and it works. It's the same principle as the old "doctrine of signatures," or "like attracting like."

When psychedelic drugs are taken in homeopathic form—where there is, say, only one ten-millionth part of the drug remaining in the solution—they can induce a change of consciousness without unduly upsetting the body chemistry. Nevertheless, I am not advising you to go playing around with them, not even in that modified form. I know it has been done in certain lodges, but personally I'm rather cautious about anything that interferes with the body's chemistry.

You can alter your consciousness by your own will, by your own self-power. You can get the pituitary gland to secrete that chemical which will open up the inner consciousness. It is done by willed disassociation—in other words, autotrance. If you read about the Golden Dawn rituals (everybody likes to read about the Golden Dawn and own the four volumes which Israel Regardie produced),[6] you have to bear in mind that there is a lot of Golden Dawn material that was never published. For instance, the flashing tablets. Flashing tablets are complimentary colors superimposed on each other. When you look at them, they "*flash*," as you might expect. And, after staring at them for a while, the flashing becomes intensified, hypnotic almost. This little exercise is said to help develop the power of clairvoyance. The Golden Dawn had the complementary colors displayed in all their lodges. You couldn't help seeing them wherever you went.

If you read the description of the vault of Christian Rosenkreutz in the Golden Dawn manuscripts,[7] you will find how these complementary colors were used. Those people working with the Golden Dawn rituals in their own lodges were constantly subjected to the influence of the flashing colors. The colors sent them into a light kind of self-hypnosis. Then, of course, things began to happen!

Remember I told you about the hypnotized subject and his imagination, how the image-building part of the mind is so great that if you tell it to see something, it will see something. The stage hypnotist would get his subject to see somebody who wasn't there, or not see someone who was there. All kinds of hallucinations like that were produced just for fun—not a nice trick to play with the personality. But that is what can be done with the hypnotized mind; it can see objectively outside itself that which is really internal. Think what that would mean if someone else could also see your innermost thoughts externalized and walking around outside you? There are many thoughts we have which we shouldn't, so it's just as well nobody sees them.

That shift of consciousness produced by autotrance is a method you can control. It's not something that works willynilly like a psychedelic drug. You can control it and make it work beneficially for you. You can say to that inner personality—"I want this particular thing to cease"—and it will do so. You can do self-healing, banish pain, and so on. It isn't always easy when you first begin because the body is strong, but with perseverance you can do it. A lot of self-healing goes on that way when a person has, unwittingly, found the secret. People hit on it unconsciously as Napoleon did. He could sit down and put himself to sleep right away. We assume he was unconsciously employing auto-trance, but we shall never know; he might have known a thing or two. Churchill had this same power of taking a catnap to order.

There are people who, when in this kind of semitrance state, can visualize vividly so that the thought forms they build are almost visible to the naked eye. It is only necessary to have a screen on which to project them, and they will be seen by other people. That is why the incense, Dittany of Crete, is burned during certain magical operations—to provide a dense, white smoke screen in which the thought pictures projected from the mind can be seen.

Creating thought forms is within the power of the magical personality, and every occultist must develop this ability, to some extent, by his or her own efforts. It's a natural power which can be used for good or ill. You can abuse it and denigrate yourself. You can use it to build negative thought forms which become so real and so definite that you surround yourself with treacherous thoughts which continually drum into you—"I can't do this. I can't do that. Fate is against me. I'm fighting a losing battle. Everything I do goes wrong." And, of course, everything does go wrong because you are using your thought power inversely. Unfortunately, a tremendous number of people do just that; they let their inner personality run riot. It's easily done but it isn't so easy to stop it. Before you can put an end to all that negative thinking, you must first come to terms with yourself.

I'm talking about this now because it is a method of the Mysteries. Fantasy, the image-building power of the mind, is the ass that carries the ark of higher consciousness. In other words, it is through using the power of fantastic imagery that you build the ark in which the higher consciousness comes to birth. Used properly, willed dissociation (autotrance) can be used to build up within yourself a faculty of thought projection, of thought control, of thought form building, which is the essence of practical magic.

Sir Francis Bacon adapted a verse from Proverbs and made it his motto, "The Glory of God is to conceal a matter. The Virtue of Man is to find it." When I read it for the first time at the age of ten, I thought that this was going to be my motto, too, and I've had it ever since. In the old days it was said there was virtue in virginity and that an animal would never attack a virgin. During the Middle Ages, the presence of a virgin was one of the prerequisites of magic; and if she wasn't a virgin, then the magic went haywire. It was another way of saying, "The power went from her." The word "virtue" means power, something active. We talk about dynamic power; and there is within each of us, a virtue, a dynamic power. When a woman touched the robe of Jesus and was healed, He said, "Who touched my clothes?"[8] He perceived that virtue had gone out from Him. He felt that power leaving Him and going into the body of the woman and healing her. I've felt it many a time myself when I've been engaged in healing work. I've felt that power going out from me.

Don't forget this: There's a big difference between hypnotism and mesmerism. In hypnotism you are dealing with a mental faculty, with mental power. In mesmerism you are actually transmitting a force, a virtue. Although it may not have been so accidental as we are given to suppose, this virtue which goes out is a very real power that Mesmer[9] stumbled upon. It may have been something given to him by his teachers; in any case, he used that power. Mesmerism is distinct from hypnotism and produces different results—although, contrariwise, it can produce the same results as hypnotism under certain conditions; and this is why the two got so beautifully mixed up.

Sir James Braid,[10] a Manchester surgeon, found that by making people stare at a small object he could produce a trance state in them, and they behaved just the same as a mesmerized subject would. Because of that, he maintained that mesmerism had nothing to do with fluids and powers going from one person to another. He opined that it was a case of straining the eye and so sending a person to sleep; in that condition, the subject would do so-and-so and such-and-such. That's quite true; nevertheless, the two forms of sleep are vastly different. But that's another line of research for those people interested in this subject, for people interested in making new discoveries about the interaction of one psyche with the psyche of another person and interested in knowing the actual powers that flow between people. Kirlian photography has already shown that a ray of light very often goes forth from a healer's hand, so the healing can no longer be termed "imagination" by the skeptic!

When you've gained that power to induce inner consciousness, when you've "gone out," as we say, into the inner consciousness, remember, you always have to come back, if only to continue earning your bread and butter! You have to come back and you have to come back wholly. Some people do leave part of themselves behind and come back looking dazed and half dead. Some of them are wonderful psychics except for the fact that they seem unable to keep their feet firmly planted on the earth. To come safely back to earth again is a technique that's essential for you to learn. You have to reintegrate and get all the flats of your personality back where they belong. It's fairly easy to unleash the girdles of the mind, but getting them back again in the same order as they were before, that's the vital part.

I repeat, and I don't apologize for doing so. Once you start experimenting with autotrance, you must make absolutely certain you come back completely to your normal state of consciousness; and once you are back, never allow yourself to slip away again into a kind of half-state that's neither here nor there. You earth (become grounded) by telling yourself firmly that you are back on the physical plane, and it helps to have something to eat and drink. You don't do a lot of talking about where you've been and what you've seen, but you make a clear, concise record in your magic diary.[11] Then you go and do something practical, something nonoccult, so that you don't drift along thinking about inner plane things; if you do, you will tend to slip back again across the divide. You have to give yourself positive suggestions all the time. It's all part of the magical art. But there it is. There's the key to all astral projection, to the workings of the inner plane.

The building of the magical personality brings us to something else: each one of us has the actor within him or her. As Shakespeare put it, so beautifully and poetically:

> All the world's a stage,
> And all the men and women merely players:
> They have their exits and their entrances;
> And one man in his time plays many parts. . . .[12]

All of us have the power to play many parts. As I said earlier, we adapt our personality to suit the person or persons we meet and talk to. But you can adapt your personality in another way. Say there is a particular quality or virtue lacking in your makeup which you desire to develop. You take that quality and embody it in suitable form in a man or woman who has been known for that particular quality or virtue, and you'll find you can get positive spiritual results. Each of the saints was a specialist in his own line so you find the saint that personifies the quality you are seeking, and you make invocation to him, or to her. You commemorate your chosen saint by remembering incidents in his or her life. It's an ancient method that was elaborated on by St. Ignatius Loyola, the founder of the Jesuit Society. He taught his people a method of using the mind which is extraordinarily effective; it's that same "composition of place" we were discussing for working magic. It's as old as the hills. I don't know where St. Ignatius got it from, but it was practiced long, long ago in Egypt and Chaldea. I think every working occultist has used it at some time or other.

It is also possible to link up with those old god forms of the past which were used to worship the Divine. We thereby commemorate something in connection with them. In this way, we forge a link with the power locked up in those ancient thought forms, thus bringing additional power into our magical workings. Using the powers of the past like that is another form of practical occultism.

Having said all this, it's only fair to warn you that you can run into trouble there. The powers of the past are past, and it is better, safer if you like, to get in touch with the powers of the present which are immediately before the powers of the future. I'll try to elucidate: What I am now saying is already in the past. It was present, but now, even as I say it, it goes into the past. The future has moved into the present which became the past. I'm working on a razor edge of consciousness all the time. What was the future half a second ago is now the past. As Francis Bacon put it: "Time *is,* and then Time *was,* and Time *would never be.*"[13] We are all working all the time on that razor edge of consciousness. So you might try looking to the future and forgetting the past. Look for the powers which are flowing in now. Because, if you haven't the experience and the know-how, you can inadvertently bring through the forces from the qliphotic sewers of the universe, and that kind of power won't do you a bit of good. If you must bring power through, bring it from the future (which is now the present, which is now the past). Anyway, before it recedes into the past, you have already drawn upon it. That is the divine power of the Logos flowing constantly into His universe, and that power can be drawn on for any legitimate purpose you like. But, when you draw upon the powers of the past, remember you are dealing with contaminated waters. And, if you try to draw power from other people, you are indulging in black magic.

Questions from the Floor and Answers

Question: Commemorating past gods and goddesses, is it useful to the present work or is that drawing back into tainted waters?

W.E.B.: As a general rule, invocation of the gods and goddesses is something which is best left alone until you have gained a good deal of control over the images within you and have some experience under your belt. You can find yourself overwhelmed by that kind of power. Those great thought forms are charged with the power of hundreds of thousands of worshippers, and it is of all grades. In the early days of the Egyptian religion, cannibalism was a part of it. The Egyptian religion wasn't always sublime and austere. There are definite traces of cannibalism, and Dion Fortune refers to these in her book *Moon Magic*. In Egypt, the Dark Isis was worshipped as well as the Bright Isis. In those days, the Dark Isis was something pretty terrible, like Kali, the eight-armed goddess of India. There was always that destructive element behind it. So it is not wise to play around with the gods and goddesses until you know exactly what you are doing. A lot of people have come unstuck with this method. It's very spectacular because you get results, but they aren't always the results you're looking for. No, it's best to leave the gods and goddesses out of it for the time being unless your temperament is such that you can do it safely. We do not dash in where angels hesitate to tread unless we are fully competent to do so. If you find you get the willies just thinking about it, leave it alone. Your own inner instinct, your own intuition, will give you the key if you give it a chance to make itself heard. That's where meditation comes in and is useful—not the pussyfoot meditation that some people go in for, the kind of meditation that wouldn't raise the skin on a rice pudding. Real meditation is darned hard work.

Question: When the pituitary gland is stimulated with the homeopathy remedy, is there, or could there be, any ill effects from it? Obviously, from what you have said, there aren't if it is done properly.

W.E.B.: Bear in mind that the pituitary gland controls all manner of things, including the birth mechanism and the building of the embryo. So never monkey round with the gland unless you have been properly trained. If you go about it the right way and don't take risks and don't use drugs, you can develop it safely. The pituitary gland will work for you. All you do is coax it into being a little more active; then when you've finished, it reverts to its former condition. But don't try and bludgeon it. You can do this with excessive meditation in this area and with breathing exercises. Don't do that! Never pick up a book on breath control and start doing breathing exercises unless you know what you are doing. You can upset yourself so thoroughly that the end isn't worth the candle.

I know of a lady who did this. She concentrated with breathing exercises upon the pituitary body to the exclusion of everything else. She got her clairvoyance all right, but she got it at the expense of a disorganized physical body. Her internal digestive mechanism went on strike. She had digestive troubles of all kinds and couldn't eat anything warm. She had to stick to a diet of cold food. Yes, she developed clairvoyance, but she paid dearly for it.

Another thing: never follow haphazard instructions. I wouldn't advise anybody to use breathing exercises on the pituitary or any other gland; for instance, there's the thyroid which governs clairaudience. If that gland is overstimulated—well, you know the thyroid type, don't you? They rapidly burn up adrenalin; they are the fiery ones always trying to boss and dominate whoever and wherever they can because the thyroid is overactive. It's not their fault, simply their misfortune.

THE
FIRE DOWN BELOW

I would like to touch briefly on qabalah and for you to consider the Tree of Life in relation to what I'm going to say: Think of the Tree and the different sephiroth upon it. At the top, we have Kether the Crown which is said to be hollow, and through that hollow Crown of Kether come the three rays of divine influence which started the whole process going. Behind Kether are the veils of negative existence depicted on the Tree diagram as a series of half circles behind, or above, Kether. They are Ain Soph Aur, the Limitless Light; Ain Soph, the Limitless, and then Ain, the Veiled Light, the No-Thing, which is the beginning of manifestation. At Ain, the unmanifest is just beginning to break through, because the emanation of the universe is held to be a gradual process, one thing following the other. From Ain Soph Aur, we've come to Kether the Crown, and from the Crown come the powers of the universe.

Immediately after the crown is formed, the next sephiroth, Chokmah, and then immediately its complementary, Binah, are formed. These are the two I want to deal with. Chokmah and Binah are the Supernal Father and the Supernal Mother in Qabalistic metaphysics. The Jews were ever reluctant to portray God in any form; nevertheless, Qabalah did portray Him and portrayed Him as male-female. If you read Genesis you will find this: "And God said, Let us make man in our image, after our likeness. . . . So God created man in his own image, in the image of God created he him; male and female created he them."[1] The translation from the Hebrew is not so clear or as accurate as it might be. In the Hebrew, you will find: "Elohim created man in Their own Image, male and female created He them." "Elohim" is a curious word; it is a male word with a female suffix. In other words, the combined male-female powers form man in their own image. The *Zohar* says: "All that which exists, all that which has been formed by the Ancient, Whose Name is Holy, can only exist through a male and female [principle]."[2]

So from Binah and Chokmah proceed the two things which make up the duality in the universe—that is, male and female, positive and negative. Upon these are superimposed all kinds of dualities, all the dualities of the world. Some assign good and evil to them, but that is wrong. All of the different dualities—light and darkness, power and love, organization and destruction, etc.—go on the Tree of Life in the complementary sephiroth.

But it is Binah and Chokmah we are concerned with at the moment. Binah, the lady of form, is Aima, the Bright Fertile Mother. She is also Aima, the Dark Sterile Mother because she can be very cruel at times. Saturn is attributed here; and Saturn, you remember, devoured his own children until he was disabused of that nasty habit and tricked into swallowing a stone. But that is another story. So, Binah can be cruel, very limiting and oppressive. So can the Great Mother; any mother can. Mother always has form. Even in prehistoric days, when mother was the housewife in the cave, it was her conservatism, her deliberate opposition to man, which made him stay in the cave instead of gallivanting about in the wild. It was she who kept the race going, nurtured the children, and was, in fact, the mother of the race. And, in order to do all that, she had to be very cruel on occasions. The tradition of the Dark Sterile Mother is built up from the past, and this is also reflected in the lunar goddesses. They, too, have that cruel side to their nature.

The Bright Fertile Mother is the lady of form on one side of the Tree, and complementing her on the opposite side, we have Chokmah, which is force. These two working together make the universe what it is. Chokmah is a power, a force; and Binah, a quality, the quality of form—force and form working together. This form of Binah is a plastic principle; it is the background of the universe. In Hindu terminology, it is called "mûlaprakriti," the

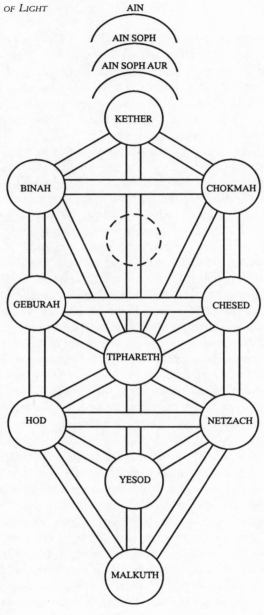

Qabalistic Tree of Life

background matter of the universe. This principle is equal to the positive Godhead; it is equally almighty, all powerful to the spirit and matter behind the scenes, as it were. Chokmah and Binah—and I repeat—each of them is equal in power. All forms can be made out of the mûlaprakriti, that ever-existing essence of space, which is Binah. Binah is the lady of all forms, and Chokmah the lord of all force.

In the universe there is always this plastic astral substance, sometimes called the Great Sea. The Great Sea is also called Marah the Bitter Sea or Mary the Bright Fruitful Sea, the Virgin Sea. The dogma of Christianity comes through from that distance far away behind Christianity. Christianity simply took up certain ideas and embodied them in a literal form. But the realities are there behind it all and Binah, the Great Mother, is the source. Everything in the universe takes its form from the principle of Binah. But she can overwhelm; she can destroy by being too formal. Binah can confine things to such an extent that they cannot move, and that is the dark sterile aspect of her. The forms are made so thick that the life underneath cannot push through. Then somebody has to break these forms (and that's the property of Geburah on the Tree of Life).

This plastic substance we've been talking about is known more generally in the West as the Astral Light, and sometimes as the Astral Sea. Hence, the titles "Virgin of the Sea" and "Star of the Sea." Although it is a plastic form substance, it is nevertheless a power, not a passive thing, but living and active; it is substance in motion, the warp and woof on the web of the universe. It is vitally important because all things depend on it. So don't forget: There are two sides to everything, the force side and the form side, and within each one of us, there are both force and form—masculine and feminine, positive and negative, light and dark, and so on.

It is said in the inner teachings that this planet of ours, like everything else, is a product of the forces of form and force. When force and form are balanced, then life appears, consciousness comes in from the middle pillar of the Tree of Life. So, wherever you have these two powers working together, you have life. Someone asked me earlier about life in the test tube. Well, the scientists don't actually make the life. All they can do is to provide the force-form balance which will enable life to manifest itself because life is always present and will push its way through wherever the opportunity is given.

This planet of ours is not dead by any means. It is a vital living thing. Mother Earth is literally a living conscious being, a great living organism. Life doesn't only extend to animals and vegetables but right down to the mineral kingdom and far below that. The mystery teachings declare that in the inner depths of the planet there is a center where all the work of the planet is done, where force and form work constantly to keep the planet working harmoniously and to allow what consciousness it has to manifest. You could call it the Heart of the World.

Now I'd like to read to you a description of the power of life from a story which, at its time of publication, gripped the whole of the Western World. The story is called *She* and was written by Sir Henry Rider Haggard. It was written in a devil of a hurry. He was a practicing lawyer at the time and yet he wrote that book in twelve weeks. He is reputed to have said that it came off his pen white hot. He didn't have to stop and think about it; it wrote itself. Rider Haggard was also a member of one of the occult fraternities, which probably explains a lot.

This is what Ayesha is saying as she shows her visitors the sights. She has just brought them to a great pillar of fire which comes and goes, and she says:

> Behold the very Fountain and Heart of Life as it beats in the bosom of the great world. Behold the substance from which all things draw their energy, the bright Spirit of the Globe, without which it cannot live, but must grow cold and dead as the dead moon. Draw near and wash you in the living flames, and take their virtue into your poor frames in all its strength—not as now it feebly glows within your bosoms, filtered thereto through all the fine strainers of a thousand intermediate lives, but as it is here in the very fount and seat of earthly Being.[3]

That's a very good description of what is described in the mystery schools as the laboratory of the Holy Ghost—the place, deep within the planet where the life force lives. When that life force goes, this planet becomes as dead as the moon is dead.

To recap, we are living on a living organism, not a dead one. The ancients were aware of this, and they acted accordingly. The Earth Mother was revered because they held her to be divine equally with the gods. She was the Great Goddess, the Lady of Form. And in the depths of this planet of ours there is this great power working in mûlaprakriti—interpenetrating the whole of the physical world, interpenetrating every one of us. Because we are children of the earth and we draw our body and our personality principles from the earth, that bright Light of the spirit of the globe enters into us. The negative power, the feminine power, is a living energy; and we draw that power up into ourselves. It is a fiery force, which in the East is called kundalini. We draw that power in and store it in a certain center of the etheric body, where it is said to be like a snake which is coiled up asleep. That kundalini shakti is sleeping in every one of us. Normally it lets through just enough energy to keep all our bodily fires stoked. When you eat and drink, you are providing the means whereby this inner fire can work. It is not the foods themselves which give you nourishment, not in the true sense. You can take in food and still be dead materially. Take a person suffering from a certain disease, who is dead by all appearances. The heart beats; the lungs pump, and that's all. But the inner fire is still working there, keeping the body going, keeping it alive. We draw from the earth's store of energy every time we breathe. We draw it in through Malkuth, which is the sephirah at the base of the feet. We draw it up through the base of the aura to the *muladhara* chakra at the base of the spine. Kundalini is the virtue of all life; if it goes, everything goes.

In the East, they have a technique of raising kundalini from its sleeping position at the base of the spine to the great chakra at the top of the head. When this is done, all the lesser fires and all the vital forces of the body are taken up, as it were, and nullified. The body becomes cold and the practitioner enters into a deep trance. Blood ceases to flow in the body, and when the final stage is reached and the kundalini force is united with the great chakra, all you will perceive of life in the yogi who is in this state is a little warmth on top of the head. Every other part of his body is icy cold; for all practical purposes he is dead. Yet, in that state of consciousness, the yogi is more alive than he ever was while in full conscious control of the physical body. All his consciousness is concentrated in the aura, that warm spot above the head. That is the same energy that flows into every one of us, the feminine power within.

The Bright Fertile Mother and the Dark Sterile Mother have been personified in mankind's worship throughout the ages. You can go right back to Magdalenian times, some fifteen thousand years before the birth of Jesus the Christ—or even further back to the Cro-Magnon race, thirty-five thousand years ago. The Cro-Magnon man is said to be the prototype of modern man and to have produced the earliest known cave paintings. Although Neanderthal man is now considered to be a mere subspecies, it has been said to go back even further, to one hundred thousand years ago. Now they've found forms of ancient life in Africa, demonstrating that we have African ancestors. Millions of years ago there were human beings, still in the semi-animal state, but human beings, nevertheless, evolving towards humanity.

In all those cultures that have been found right back to the Cro-Magnon and the Neanderthal man, you find that the Great Goddess has been worshipped. In fact, in some of the civilizations, the Great Mother was predominant and worshipped at the expense of the Great Father. In matriarchal civilizations, the men were simply an accessory after the fact. And that matriarchy has persisted all through the world in various ways. Those legendary Amazons of classic times, the female warriors who invaded Attica, were a matriarchal community.

When the Australian aborigines were first discovered, it was found that they worshipped a great principle who was unknown and unseen but all-powerful and the creator of all things. Under him were the god and goddess who carried out his will in the universe. But, when it came down to practical issues, the god had been discarded almost entirely. The unknown god remained behind the scenes. The lesser god was discarded and the goddess elevated—so much so that the natives didn't realize or understand and would not accept that a child had to be conceived by two parents. They didn't believe that the man had anything to do with it at all, and they treated him accordingly. He was an accessory to bring in the grub and generally look after things. It was the goddess through the woman who produced the child and who endowed it with intelligence. The goddess was very important in that ancient civilization.

The Australian aborigines were in the background of civilization. Certain instinctive habits indicate that they were at one time a cultured and civilized race far back behind the period of matriarchy and back behind that again. All this has been discovered through anthropological research.

A big blot on our copybook is the fact that, not so very long ago, white men organized gangs of beaters and marksmen to flush out and kill the Tasmanian natives for sport, Anglo-Saxon sport. There's a lot of hatred directed at us, some unfairly, but there's a good deal for which we are responsible and rightly deserve that resentment.

The war of the sexes is a very old one. It isn't confined to modern times, to women's lib. The Mother principle has always been regarded under the two aspects of the Bright Fertile Mother and the Dark Sterile Mother—in other words, the White Isis and the Dark Isis. Isis was the prototype of most of the goddesses of the Mediterranean basin; she was worshipped throughout. There were a Babylonian and a Chaldean goddess with the same attributes, and the worship was so similar they could have gone into each other's temples and not have known the difference.

That worship of the Great Mother developed a very efficient system of yoga. (Incidentally, its proper pronunciation is "joga," as in "conjugal." Conjugal means the same thing because yoga means Union.) Although it was practiced by both men and women, kundalini yoga was founded mainly on a feminine basis. There are women yogis, or "yoginis" as they are called, and some of them are very efficient. There have always been women who have followed this line and who have learned to evoke from within themselves the shakti which we call kundalini. Of kundalini it is said, "She gives wisdom to the wise and bondage to fools." I know this to be true because she gave bondage to this particular fool.

When I was in India, I worked with kundalini and I succeeded in arousing the kundalini energy in me. Afterward, I rued my precociousness for a very long time. I can speak of that time feelingly because it knocked me back years in my career. Kundalini is a very real force—a very real power, a magical power of tremendous potency. When you start mucking about with kundalini, you are asking for trouble. Although I was working with a group of Hindu occultists, it didn't stop me making private experiments, twisting the directions, taking short cuts. It's something we all do. We all think we can improve on nature.

On this planet of ours there are what are called psychic or sacred centers. In Britain we have Glastonbury, Iona, Lindisfarne, and scores of others dotted about the landscape. These sacred centers are connected with ley lines, and it's the same all over the world. America has its share of ley lines. Europe has them too. They can be found all over the globe. It is a theory held by many occultists, and confirmed by many others, that ley lines are actually the lines of power in the aura of the earth and that along those ley lines the power flows. There's a very interesting semiscience growing up in connection with ley lines, but there is a lot more still to be learned about them. We're only scratching at the surface.

Now, the power which flows through the ley lines and the power which flows through the kundalini chakra is alchemical power, that same power which changes base metals into gold. Alchemy has always been regarded as being a kind of moonshiny business, changing metals into gold! Yet there have been scores of experiments recorded of it having been done. But, because it sounded so impossible, everybody declared it must be a fraud. It couldn't be done; no one could transmute metals into gold. It was contrary to natural law, it was said.

But there is nothing in the process contrary to natural law. Natural law is always natural and will continue to be so. Anything checked against it either agrees with natural law, or else it doesn't exist. If you can prove by experiment that it is possible to change one metal to another, then it can be done. We know for instance, that radium, a radioactive element, breaks down to helium and lead as it emits its radiations. These are three elements which were once held to be absolutely incapable of being changed. Nature can transmute metals from one to another; and what nature can do, man can do also. And this is the way of it: kundalini shakti is a power in a plastic substance which is prematter. Those of you who have read de la Warr's books about radionics[4] will remember that the positive is a prematter in which disease appears at the etheric level before it is diagnosed in the physical body. Kundalini works in the prematter on the etheric levels; and, as all substances and all elements have their bases in this prematter, they can be approached from that angle if you know how to adjust and to direct Kundalini.

When the alchemist claimed to be able to change base metals into gold, he had first to change his own nature so that he could develop that kundalini shakti, and, through that shakti, he was able to affect the prematter behind any element he liked—be it gold, silver, or whatever. That same power is innate within everyone. You have it and I have it; but because of the tremendously difficult task of regenerating the personality, not one in ten million people should ever try to be alchemists. It is a very arduous path. But it has been done in China, in India, and in the West. There is always someone trying to have a go at the "great work." And there is sufficient evidence to prove that it has been done and can be done.

Think what would happen if you broadcast to all and sundry the fact that you could transmute base metal into gold. Our national debt is a tidy little sum. Think of how it would be if some unscrupulous prime minister were to get hold of you quietly and put you through the equivalent of the Inquisition until you agreed to turn base metal into gold. It occurred more than once in the Middle Ages. There's the story of Dr. John Dee and his pal Sir Edward Kelly.[5] They found themselves in the castle of a certain nobleman who demanded that they change base metal into gold—or else! They were kept there as prisoners for quite a time. Edward Kelly did escape and broke his leg in the process. Dee got away eventually.

Once the whisper got around that you could change base metal into gold, then every prince and every potentate and every chancellor of the exchequer would be after your blood. Yes, even today!

Towards the end of the fourteenth century, Nicholas Flamel,[6] a notary living in Paris, bought a second-hand book entitled the *Book of Abraham the Jew.* It was a strange book with lots of curious illustrations. At the time, Flamel didn't understand a word of it and spent many years studying both the text and the diagrams. He even painted some of the pictures on the walls of his house. The book was, of course, about alchemy—with instructions for turning base metal into gold. It wasn't until he found an adept of the Mysteries to instruct him that Flamel began to understand the sacred teachings in the book. The adept died; but Flamel, with the help of his wife Perrenella, did eventually transmute base metal into gold, and more than once. The Flamels endowed many churches and hospitals before it came to the notice of the authorities that Nicholas Flamel, one time struggling notary, was now a rich man and giving away gold by the fistful. The couple were warned in time before officials could pick them up, and they made their escape. Had they been caught, they would have been tortured until they revealed their secret (not that it would have done their torturers much good).

Flamel is reputed to have had some of the alchemical designs from the book painted on an arch of St. Innocent's Churchyard in Paris. There he concealed the whole formula for transmuting base metal into gold.

Other alchemists were Paracelsus, Roger Bacon and his friend, Raymond Lully, and the fabulous Count de St. Germain.

The power of man over the elements of nature is what it all amounts to. Man has this latent power not only over the elements and animals in the Garden of Eden but over everything in the Garden of Eden. We have lost that control at present, but it can be regained. Then we shall be able to transmute base metal into gold and to evoke from the astral records of the past those things of beauty and of truth and of joy which have been lost through mankind's foolishness. We can restore all that loveliness to life again because, like the Source of All Life, we also are universe-builders although, as yet, we are unaware of our wonderful powers.

Kundalini power enables us to have control over what we call inanimate nature. Not that there is anything really inanimate. There is life in all matter; nothing is dead. There are simply degrees of life: it's in a trance in the rock; it sleeps in the vegetable; it awakens in the animal; and it becomes consciousness in mankind, the One Life behind all things. So you see we carry a lot of potentiality within us.

The laboratory of the Holy Ghost abides in the center of the planet. The fire of life circulates through the entire globe and comes out at the sacred centers in great gushes of power. One day, in Benares, I stood looking into the brilliant sky of midsummer. It was very hot, and the sky was absolutely clear. I remember then seeing a great flood of life pouring up from the earth in a jet of power to some forty or fifty feet in the air before dispersing. That was one of the Fountains of Hecate as they are designated in some of the older books. And you can find those Fountains of Hecate here in Britain, in places like Glastonbury Tor, that are emanating power from the life force of the planet. It is that same life force manifesting as kundalini shakti that is taken up and stored by us and released in dribs and drabs throughout our whole system by a wonderful automatic process. If, as a species, we learn to govern that process and to increase the flow of kundalini in our bodies, we can begin to change the nature of our bodies to such an extent that ultimately (which won't be for thousands of years) we come to a point when the physical body is responsive to kundalini shakti through its every atom. And then, if we want to walk through a wall, we resolve the physical body into prematter and we walk through the wall without obstruction. It is what the theologians call, "the resurrection body," the body which walks out from the tomb, which can walk through walls. That resurrection body which we have within us is the glorified Solar Body.

When the physical body is changed into that resurrection body—as it is destined to be—all the physical power of the physical body will be at the service of the freed spirit who can materialize at will in any place. He will be able to take his body on any plane he wishes, including the physical. There are great masters of life, the true masters, who have realized that secret which is in every one of us. They can reconstitute their physical bodies so that they become temporarily immaterial. No, I'm not talking nonsense; there are authentic cases of this happening. In time this material universe and everything that is of material substance will become immaterial. The whole of the universe will pass into a condition of no matter. In the East it is called "pralaya," a condition wherein no life can manifest because there is no form by which it can manifest. The goddess is sleeping; the universe sleeps; all material things are no more. Perhaps those black holes we now hear so much about are a phenomenon in which matter is being disintegrated and formed back into prematter. It rather looks that way.

The time will come when all physical life has gone, the inner planes have gone, and all that remains is the Eternal Spirit brooding over the creation that was and which has now reached its fruition, the fruits thereof absorbed within Itself. Then, in the far distant future, there will come a time in the dawn of the gods when the life of Kether flows once more, and Binah is reestablished; when the plastic substance of the universe again comes into manifestation. All the old forms, all the old knowledge of the Logos now locked up in that wallet which the fool of the tarot carries, all that knowledge will come into manifestation again. All the sons and daughters of the One Life who have evolved in this universe will return as universe builders. We shall be the morning stars who sing together for joy as we begin to work together in cooperation with the Logos in His new task in the new Universe in a realm of new ideals and new conceptions of reality. That is the occult background to all our work. When you think about it, it is a little better than believing we are going to an eternal heaven to sing psalms and play harps or to a spot where you are tormented with red-hot pokers!

Human beings have a greater dignity than they realize. This is why any attempt to use magical work for the aggrandizement of the personality or for the hurt of other people is so evil. It goes against the very purpose of the Universe. When we do that, we are going against ourselves, damaging ourselves. There is a school of philosophy which says, "So long as I don't hurt anybody else I'm quite all right. I can do what I like so long as I don't hurt other people." But it isn't all right.

We hurt other people the minute we start thinking that way.

We then begin to affect other people to their detriment—"For none of us liveth to himself, and no man dieth to himself."[7] As John Donne wrote:

> No man is an Island, entire of itself. . . . Any man's death diminishes me, because I am involved in Mankind; And therefore never send to know for whom the bell tolls; It tolls for thee.[8]

We are all linked together. When we start monkeying about with the magical laws or when we try to be laws unto ourselves, we are misusing the power, that divine power which we have as children of the Most High. And sooner or later we pay for it.

We've talked about earth and its ley lines, and now we come to ourselves and our own personal ley lines. I don't know if any of you have ever seen the body of a person when he or she is in astral projection. I've seen it a good many times. Linked to the astral body is a line of light—the silver cord, as it is called. If you examine it closely, you will find it is made up of innumerable lines of light twisted together, and those strands of light come from every cell in the body. Every cell in our bodies has that line of light emanating from it. These lines subdivide and permeate every molecule of our bodies. All the lines are linked together in this silver cord, which again goes to the etheric double. That etheric double is the matrix into which the physical body has been built. All the vital forces, all the health forces—everything flows from the etheric double into the physical body. You will find these lines of force throughout the entire body. Every part of the etheric body, interior and exterior, has one of these lines of light coming from it. They come forth from certain centers in the same way that the force emanates from the sacred centers of the earth.

Though, generally speaking, the silver cord extends from the top of the head, it can emanate from other parts of the body, depending on the particular race—from the solar plexus, the back of the head, the front of the head, or from the throat center. There are innumerable lines of light extending from the physical body to the etheric double.

When we know what we are about, we can assist that etheric

double in its work by bringing currents of force along these ley lines and distributing them in the physical body. In so doing we can revitalize and recharge our batteries. One very simple method is to sit with your back against an ordinary pine tree and let your etheric aura (etheric and aura overlap a little) lean towards the tree. If you sit there passively for a while, you'll find you get a real charge of vitality, because along your human ley lines are flung the forces of the vegetable ley lines of the pine tree. You are joining the two systems of communication together and actually getting a flow from one to the other. If you're ever feeling really bushed, devitalized, try it—that is, if you can get close to a pine tree in this modern, civilized world! There are other trees which emanate different influences. There's a whole psychic science about it dating back to the Middle Ages.

With time, patience, and meditation, you can learn to manipulate the forces within your own self. There is a technique of breathing and concentration which helps to arouse kundalini, but it can be dangerous, very dangerous, unless it is done under the supervision of those who know what they are about. It's nice to have that tiger of power, but when the tiger can turn round and bite you at any given moment, then it isn't so good. That fire of kundalini can take chunks out of you, both physically and mentally. I would not advise you to follow the instructions of any book or any person on how to arouse kundalini, unless you know for the gospel truth that that person has been properly trained and knows what he or she is doing.

Kundalini has come in manageable doses to many students after a time—after they have spent time developing self-discipline, after meditation, and the sheer hard slog of regenerating the personality. And don't forget concentration, that's very important. (Kim's Game[9] is excellent training for that.) You need absolute razor-sharp concentration when you are working kundalini, because it only needs a lapse in your thinking, a break in your concentration, and the power goes where your thinking goes, and you're in trouble. Rampaging kundalini can disturb every function in your body. It can even kill. It is best to regard it as one of those things that you have; but, for the present, you're keeping it locked away in that little wallet on your back.

The tarot cards can be specially illuminating and Paul Foster Case, in his book on the tarot, gives a lot of valuable information which can help you to use the tarot to your spiritual advantage. The tarot is attuned to most things relating to the Mysteries. It isn't simply a filing cabinet; it is much, much more. There are people who devote their entire lives to the tarot. I don't mean for fortune—telling purposes but for the deeper occult meaning which is hidden in the cards.

Questions from the Floor and Answers

Question: Do you think self-hypnosis can be used beneficially in conjunction with meditation?

W.E.B.: Yes, definitely, but it has to be done properly. If you just play around and disregard its laws, you won't get very far. Self-hypnosis, or autotrance, is a tricky business. You can induce it and get going very nicely. And then, for some reason or other, you repudiate it, put a block on something. Then the next time you try to induce it, you find you can't. The block you've put up is still there, and until you unblock it, you're stuck. But once you get the knack—and that means obeying its laws—it can be useful in many different ways. It is marvellous what you can do with it. Self-hypnosis can help with health conditions or when you're taking an exam and want a little extra factual information. If you're an artist, it can revive your artistic talent.

You can also build up your visualizing power which is always helpful in magical work. There's a little trick of the mind I can do, and you can learn it, too, with practice: I can visualize a silver pyramid, about nine inches square at the base and tapering upwards to about a foot high, perhaps a little less. I can visualize and see it now objectively as though it were actually in position on that table. It is a power some artists possess, to be able to project a picture onto canvas and then paint in the picture. I knew a child that had the same ability; she drew these marvellous silhouette pictures. When I asked her about them, she said, "I think and then I draw lines on my think." A very good way of describing it. Many people have that particular power of the mind and you can develop it with autotrance. But it has to be clear-cut, precise thinking; and then you get a clear-cut image.

When you start meditating properly and building the thought forms in magical work, the forms are no longer inside your head. They are seen objectively, outside yourself. You can call it hallucination if you like, so you have to be careful. When you've finished your magical work you must banish those forms properly, get rid of them. Otherwise, you'll go around with a lot of semivisible thought forms and you won't know whether you're coming or going. But it can be done. It helps tremendously in occult work if you have that visualizing power strongly established because, as I keep on telling you, it is fantasy that carries the ark in the mysteries.

Question: Can you tell me if there is any relationship between alchemy and the transmutation of metals and the philosophers' stone?

W.E.B.: Yes. The philosophers' stone was simply a convenient point from which to work. The effort of making the stone aroused in the alchemist the powers which we have been talking about, those powers of transmutation. He was able to formulate and materialize the stone as a doorway to those powers, and he could turn that philosophers' stone to healing the sick or whatever he liked, and it worked. It changed base metals into gold, prolonged his life, and so on. But it's not the stone itself that does it. The stone was just a handy focussing point. The real power was in the mind of the alchemist, in his personality; and it still is. You can have the philosophers' stone and you can change base metal into gold. But all that is happening is the very thing we've been talking about. It's the enflamed mind and purified personality of the alchemist bringing through powers and forces which already exist and work in nature. There's an old saying that nature unaided fails. Nature goes a long way on her own, gets so far, and then sticks. But when human will and human power come to her aid, nature can be advanced beyond her natural limit and become supernormal. And mankind has the power to do just that; in time he will learn how to use that power, but just at present, it's a wicked kind of world in which to let that power run loose.

It seems that when some of the scientists have a go at telepathy, they have a one-track mind. They can only think of using it telepathically to influence dolphins to carry a charge of high explosives on their backs and dash themselves against another nation's ships. That is the scientific mind at work. We've discovered something; now let's see what we can kill with it.

Man is a curious animal, the most destructive and predatory animal the planet knows. Very few animals prey upon their own kind. Man is the exception. When we think of that, the occult possibilities, and where we stand, we wonder sometimes if we are right to try anything at all along occult lines. On the other hand, if we don't, the reverse side gets out of balance. Evil is given too much rein. You don't oppose wickedness by simply sitting down and letting it run over you. You accept it and find ways and means of dealing with it. You don't just let it run amok. That is the trouble with some idealists; they like to quote Robert Browning—"God's in His heaven—All's right with the world!"[10] And it's God's world, they tell you. Yes, it is God's world, and we're doing our best to muck it up.

Question: What you are saying then is that the baseness of man can be transmuted into the gold of the Divine.

W.E.B.: Exactly, that is the essence of the entire operation. By doing that he gains the power to transmute base metal into gold and to alter the chemical and atomic composition of substances. He learns to reform substance and remake it according to his will. But it is all based upon the transmutation of himself. He has to accomplish that transmutation before he can effect transmutation of anything else. So it isn't something you can write down in a book and sell for a few dollars.

Training the Personality:

ADONAI INTERNA

My title for this talk is "Adonai Interna," which means the internal Lord. "Adonai" is the Lord, the internal Lord, the God within.

Running through all the talks I have given there has been the theme that we are the children of the Most High. We are not simply worms of the earth, but complex sons and daughters of the Absolute. There are bits and pieces in us that come from the earth, and other bits and pieces which come from the starry heavens. Now I want to talk a little about the occult anatomy of mankind.

First, we have a physical body. We know we have because we can see it and handle it, unlike the other bodies which are invisible to normal sight. We then have the etheric body, the form upon which the physical body is based. In the older literature on occult science it was known as the astral body. This has caused a lovely lot of misinformation because the astral body is something quite different. We will come to it in a minute. In the old days, the astral body was thought of as the etheric double, the matrix, the real body upon which all this arrangement of cells, bones, and muscles is built. The astral body was thought to be the archetypal physical body, which is the etheric double. All kinds of names have been given to it. In German it is the *dopplegänger*, in Hindu, *prânamâyakosha* or vehicle of *Prâna* (*Prâna* means vitality). But the astral body and the etheric double are two distinct bodies, and you have to be careful not to confuse the two.

Beyond that, we have our emotions and our thinking, our general day-to-day thinking. The astral body is sometimes appropriately called the emotional body because it is the seat and center of our emotions. It is affected by sensation and feeling and, of course, desire. Then comes the mental body. The mental body has two levels of consciousness, the higher and what you might call the lower, or in more sophisticated terminology, the abstract mind and the concrete mind. The concrete mind is the intellectual function and deals with objective matters and ordinary everyday thinking. The abstract mind (the higher mental body) is the intuitional faculty and creative urge. It is through the higher mental body that the Logos is contacted. Both our emotions and our general thinking can only be generated through some kind of substance; they cannot work in a vacuum. So we are working in what is sometimes called the astral light, in substance behind matter—in a certain type of substance or a certain order of substance called emotional or mental, as the case may be. Because no one thinks without engendering emotion, thought and emotion mingle together; and that is known as the *kama manasic*. "Kama" means desire. (Don't get confused with karma which is the law of cause and effect.) Kama has an important function in our makeup; it is the driving force without which we should be like cabbages. But desire has to be controlled and directed into the proper channels. "Manas" means to think, to ponder, and to reflect—mental activity. So we have this body of astral substance adapted for the use of our emotions and commonly called the astral body or the *kama manasic* body because it is also adapted for mental activity. Beyond that is the higher mental self which works in its own body, in the substance of its own plane. The mental body is an important part of the personality because it controls both the astral and physical bodies to a greater or lesser extent, depending on individual development.

Let's look again at this lower quaternary—the physical, the etheric, the astral, and the mental. Remember that each body is dependent on the one above; this means that each body is negative to the one above it and positive to the one below. All of them are concerned with the world and with evolution, with the evolution of our lives and with our general conduct in the world and our ultimate fate. For instance, our ordinary mind (concrete mind) is shaped and influenced from childhood, from the time we were born. It is molded by both our good and bad experiences, and so we build into ourselves a false mind based on experiences and our interpretation of them. More often than not, we misinterpret events and we build into our astral body little things which don't always agree with one another. Thus, the astral body is badly constructed because it is continually being fed with the wrong material. In the same way, if someone ate all the most unsuitable foods, the physical body would begin to protest. The astral body does this, too, in its own way. The etheric body is the link between the physical and astral bodies and that link is the mold on which the physical body is built. It confines and limits the physical body; it keeps it within the frame of the pattern. Otherwise, our physical substance would never cease to grow, and we could very well end up with fingers and toes six feet long!

It has been said that the real physical body is the etheric double and that the physical body we have today came later as an after-thought. We fell so low that we picked up an animal body which should never have been. That is the tradition behind a certain oc-cult school. The etheric double might also be called the magnetic body, or vital body; all the vital forces flow through it, and it is recharged by solar energy while we sleep. Thus, the lower quater-nary of the physical, mental, astral, and etheric forms the self as we know it.

Within that self is the center from which we think. Very often we think from the emotional center. Quite a number of Celtic people do that, and they will tell you that they think from the solar plexus. Their thinking is emotional to the highest degree. But, generally speaking, we think from our heads because we have evolved certain mental faculties beyond emotion which work in the higher centers in the head and in the brain. Now these faculties are connected to the false ego or the empiric ego, which we have constructed within ourselves and hypnotized ourselves into believ-ing. This is not the true self, because it has been built on erroneous information. It doesn't really come to grips with the real things of life at all. Therefore, it can cause all kinds of confusion because we cannot discriminate properly from those lower centers of the con-crete mind and emotional body. We do not have all the faculties there.

Behind the lower quaternary is the higher mental body, and behind the higher mental body is the causal body. Behind that again is the Buddhic body, the highest vehicle we possess. "Vehicle" is a better word, because it's nothing like a physical body. The Buddhic vehicle is the last form we use. We come through from the lower centers to the higher part of ourselves where form is left behind. Then we are no longer form creatures. We've become formless; but in that formlessness, we possess the power to organize ourselves into any form we wish—be it physical, etheric, astral, or mental. It is part of our evolutionary progress that we should eventually come to that state. Beyond the Buddhic body is the ground of the soul, known in the East as Atman. It is that part where the Infinite impinges upon the finite self. Just as the higher mental side of ourselves is brooding over the astral mental, the ground of the soul is the brooding influence of spirit over the self below; that is to say that the self, the lower self, is brooded over all the time by the influence of the higher self. And that higher self is, in its turn, brooded over by the influence of the Atman or the monad, the spirit in each one of us.

There is no immediate connection between the three sections of ourselves; the monad appears to be distinct from the individual and the individual distinct from the personality. We are split into sections and our evolution is designed to heal the splits, to get rid of the divisions between those three aspects of our nature. We have divorced our nature from our self because we have made ourselves feel that we are insufficient, that we are less than we should be. And because of the marvelous power of our minds, we have hypnotized ourselves into believing this and acting accordingly. Tell a man under hypnotism that he is in the deep end of a swimming pool, and he will immediately start trying to swim.

In the same way, we have hypnotized ourselves into believing that this lower ego, this self down below, is all important. But it is not. For the time being, it is of relative importance because it helps us to establish ourselves as individual beings. We have to gather bodies around us. Bodies always involve this notion of a false ego. The false ego is a way of looking at things, and because of that, it limits our personality. Yet, all the time we are endeavoring to unfold that personality, to evolve it. As we continue to do that, our outlook becomes wider, broadens out. Consequently, we begin to understand ourselves better. And with understanding comes enlightenment. Finally, the day dawns when we have attained self-knowledge, perfect self-knowledge. Then the true self comes into manifestation.

But, as I said, the development of the personality proceeds haphazardly. We gain by our experiences in the world. We make mistakes and learn not to make them again; but generally speaking, it is a haphazard process. Nobody takes us by the hand and steers us comfortably along the right path. Even if somebody said, "Walk along the old, tried and tested paths, and you will find rest for your soul," the chances are we should ignore the injunction because we have that persnickety bit in us. We don't listen; we want to be different. That contrariness is in the whole of the personality, all because of that false ego and its false images always trying to organize everything around itself. But, we are not that false ego. We are that which lies behind it, and the day will come when we have to relinquish that false ego. Still, because it is related to all the lovely things we have chosen for ourselves, we tend to hang on to it. We hang on to those illusory images because they agree with what we think we want. They have nothing to do with the reality or the true path we should be following. Because of that, we only see that part of ourselves we have achieved by unwitting self-hypnosis; because we want to deceive ourselves, to feel this, to think that; because it panders to our self-aggrandizement, to the fact that we think we are that someone built up by the false personality. And we're stuck with that false image. We have to work alongside it, run with it through life until the time comes when we have to lay aside our physical sheath and separate our personality from the physical body.

When we leave the physical plane for the inner planes we find there are a whole lot of things we have to jettison. We need to get rid of as much of the lumber as we possibly can before we pass through those pearly gates. If you take it with you, then you still have to get rid of it. It all has to go.

There is a purgation, a cleansing of our personality, and we learn to retain only that part which is good, beautiful, and true. We keep only that which is real, which is a reflection of the divine idea. That purgation on the inner planes is a very definite thing; and if you ever have communication with the other side, you will find that quite a lot of people whom you thought in earth life to be on a very high level are not so high after all. They had built into their personality traits of character which now have to be discarded, and it can be a painful process, especially where that false ego has been developed very strongly. It's no easy matter to persuade it to get rid of the rubbish. However, unless you do discard it, you hang about on the lower planes for ages. You can't progress. You're like a diver weighed down; and unless you get rid of some of the weight, you won't float to the top.

It is a lot more difficult to rid yourself of the rubbish on the other side than it is here. If you want to reform your lower self and get it trained, now's the time to do it. Don't wait till you get to the other side. What you can do in dense physical plane matter is not managed quite so easily in the mobile flashing substances of the inner planes. There's no resistance to work against. With self-discipline and perseverance in one year of earth life, instead of fifty years of astral life, you can purify a good deal of your personality. It pays to do your purgation while you are still in the physical body. That is what the mystic is always shouting about. He says, "Never mind about anything else. You have to purge yourself of your sins."

Sins are really transgressions, and to transgress means "to go across." You are firing at a target but aiming wrongly, and you go across the target rather than on it. You transgress. We wander from the path, and that is sin. We would not sin if we knew how to aim straight, but we don't. It's something we have to learn. The more we can learn on the physical plane about how to control our emotional and mental reactions, the less clutter we shall take with us when we change houses.

You don't want a lot of clutter when you pass to the inner planes. Let go while you are still here, and then you won't have to undergo all that painful purgation. It's painful for this reason: When you try to cleanse yourself from your sins of admission and commission on this plane, you have the dense physical body to hold you in line on the low vibration of the physical (not low in the moral sense but low in the sense that it is on a lower octave of vibration). Therefore, you can assess your shortcomings and deal with them accordingly and with relatively less agony.

When you arrive on the other side, you will find that in the fine volatile matter of the inner planes, your transgressions take charge of themselves. They materialize in front of you. You have to deal with them as if they were actual living things standing there before you in all their hideousness. If you've been guilty of utter selfishness, you could find yourself imprisoned by that selfishness, locked into it by the appearance of solid iron bars all around you. On the inner planes, when you think of a thing, it is immediately there before you. Don't forget that! You have to train yourself to absorb all that unworthiness. You can see how imperative it is for you to do your sorting out while you are still in the dense physical body where this mobile element doesn't enter into it. Otherwise, you are storing up a lot of troublesome work for yourself. In due course, you have to undergo that purging whether you like it or not, either here or there, before you can go on to a higher level.

When you get to the other side, there will always be something remaining in your personality that needs purging because not one of us is perfect. When all the negative qualities of your personality have been assimilated, you are ready to move on to a higher level where you begin to come into the realms of your true self. You have "risen on the planes," as it is said. As you ascend to the higher planes, you begin to shed the old ideas and a new kind of consciousness takes over—new thought and new images that you had never experienced before, fresh pictures, new forms of beauty, and so on. Strange memories begin to creep in, and you wonder where they've come from. You enter a condition in which you have more or less finished with the personality. But you have taken from that personality all the lessons you learned and incorporated them in the higher memory, that higher consciousness where all the memories of all past lives are stored. You have purged your personality of all that was unbalanced and negative. All that remains of the abandoned personality is a kind of astral detritus, or shell, as it is sometimes called, which eventually disintegrates. And you have returned to where? To the higher self, to the true ego, to the true self? Then, you are in what in the East is called *devachan*—heaven, if you like.

You remain there until the time comes when you desire to go forth again. That time will come; the desire will arise. Many spiritualists say, "Oh, I never want to come back to this earth again"; nevertheless, they can't help themselves. They won't return as that same personality, but they will come back because the spirit within says, "I am going to conquer. I am going to conquer matter," because behind our inner spirit is the spirit of the Eternal Will and that Eternal Will is saying, "I, the Spirit will conquer matter." It is that God-impulse within us which leads us in turn to say, "I too will conquer matter." That urge brings us back into matter to conquer or to rescue it.

In part of the Golden Dawn ritual, you find these words: "I am the rescuer of matter." What does this mean? Well, every bit of matter that comes within our orbit and passes through our bodies is stamped with our individuality. We impress our life force upon it; we alter it. Either we increase its vibrations or we lower them. No part of matter passes through our body which is not altered in its passage. For good or worse, we are constantly remolding matter. Either we are degrading it, or else we're rescuing it. It is a continual process. This was expressed in the ancient glyph of the circle on the cross which is the basis of the Rosicrucian cross. The Calvary cross, when it is folded in a certain way, forms a cube, the cube of matter. The Calvary cross represents sacrifice, suffering, confinement, and limitation. The cosmic cross symbolizes the spirit immersed in matter, sacrificed in matter, crucified in matter. Spirit has to learn by raising matter, lifting it up and controlling it. It is one of the laws of the universe; the spirit effects matter through the different selves which we use. Each personality we take on is a tool in the hand of our spirit self to rescue matter while at the same time developing the spirit. Spirit and matter go together like the left hand and the right hand. We cannot lift ourselves without also lifting matter. We are continu-

ally uplifting the whole globe infinitesimally, little by little, or push-
ing it down, little by little. That is our evolutionary task. As time goes
on, the mind of mankind will more and more consciously raise or
lower matter until that day when spirit will have conquered matter,
conquered it in the sense that it has raised it to the higher level.

In ancient Egypt they used to bake a little circular cake with a
cross on it. That confection was called "the cake of the day the
gods come unto us," that is, when spirit shall have conquered matter and matter shall be subservient to spirit. Then, the Eternal will
finally triumph and God shall be all in all.

This goal has been the background of all religious systems. It is a
possibility we believe to be true. We have been told by those who
went before us, who were told by those who went before them, and
again by those who went before them. This teaching goes right back
to legendary Atlantis, right back to the time when animal man first
came under the control of the lords from Venus (as it is told in the
oldest Hindu scriptures on record). These lords, highly advanced
spiritual beings, came from Venus. They came in the equivalent of
great spaceships to the region where the Gobi Desert now lies, where
the land was then fruitful. The lords began to organize and teach
animal man. He hadn't evolved then to the thinking stage. He could
only feel emotionally, and the lords of Venus induced in that animal
man, by telepathic means, the power to think. As it is recorded in
the books, "They gave him a mind." Then animal man began to
think as well as feel; he began to evolve. A few of those great ones
remained with the infant humanity to guide and guard it along its
upward path. That's the ancient Hindu story, the story of the de-
scent of the lords of Venus, the beginning of thinking life on this
planet when the animal emotional life was given a chance to think.

As we understand it, that process goes on all the time. There are
always perfected spiritual beings on this earth working to guide
mankind. The unidentified-flying-object people believe that some
of them are still coming in their spaceships as they did many eons
ago from Venus. To me, that is something which must remain
open. I am not a UFO fan; nevertheless I keep an open mind. Carl
Jung, in writing a book on the subject of flying saucers, pointed out

that there is a time when all of humanity is looking for a savior to come—either the return of the Christ, the Second coming, or for a new avatar who will save us from ourselves, rescue us from all the sin, wickedness, and destruction we have brought upon ourselves.[1] For some people, their psychology subconsciously demands the fantasy of a spaceship carrying an advanced spiritual being or beings.

Because we are looking out subconsciously for that spiritual help and rescue, the mind of man projects itself on to anything likely. He can't project it on to a teacher because teachers are out of fashion, but he can latch on to an unidentified flying object up there in the sky. He presupposes that if they are there, they must contain people, people who want to help us. But, if there are such people, they may not necessarily be looking to help us; they may even be dangerous. You read science fiction stories about how an earthman goes forth in his space ship and crushes alien civilizations on other stars, but the boot could be on the other foot: there could be alien civilizations wanting to overcome or eliminate us. Because we are looking for something to clutch onto, many people believe in flying saucers—not because they've seen them, not because they have any rational evidence about them, but simply because they feel it should be so, a sort of wishful thinking. We feel it is only right we should be delivered from the effects of our own follies, that God should step in and send someone to rescue us from our sins and errors; and we project those feelings of insecurity onto the UFO. A great deal of the UFO stuff is simply that. I'm not saying it all is because, as I've said earlier, I like to keep an open mind on the subject. I've read a good deal about it from the psychological angle and can understand why certain people feel the need to project their desire for spiritual protection onto UFOs. Nevertheless, I equally believe there are great spirits of power, love, and wisdom who are trying to help us—trying to uplift us to something better—but they don't go about it in that spectacular fashion.

Because these great spiritual beings don't appear before us on a roll of thunder and with a great flapping of wings, we cannot imagine them or believe in them or their work. They don't appear and say, "Behold, I am the Great Archangel Whatsit! I have come to

save you." That is not their way. Because they don't show themselves, we refuse to believe they exist.

Should someone rather ordinary looking happen along and offer
help and advice for our problems, we don't fall over ourselves to
take their advice. We think our particular problem is special and
unique, so how can such a nondescript person be of any help to us.
Perhaps we should have listened to the advice of that ordinary person; perhaps the Great Archangel Whatsit has come to us in the
form of that person who offered us help. Because we didn't recognize him in that guise, we rejected him and his counsel. Many
messengers of light, many disciples of the masters, are rejected because they are not glamorous enough for our liking.

When you come to think about it, we're a wicked lot of devils
really; yet, in another way, we're a silly lot of children. We are
blinded by our own prejudices; we are blinded by our emotions,
blinded by our self-opinionated ideas. And because we've created
these ideas, because we've experienced these emotions, we can't
bear to let them go. We love them; we're possessive about them;
they are ours, and so we won't let go of our *little self,* because we're
afraid that if we do, everything will collapse. We are like a child
refusing to be born, refusing to leave our snug beautiful paradise for
the strange world outside the womb. We fear to let go and move
forward because all the time we're hugging the past. Ultimately the
child must be born. It cannot help itself, and when it gets into the
world, it finds the world isn't the alien place it dreaded. We, too,
must learn to let go. The old proverb says, "Let go and let God."
Just that! When we eventually let go and let the God within us take
charge, we find we never lose anything of value. We may forfeit a
lot of foolish things, things which are no good to us; but we never
lose anything of real value. That is the key to occultism: Letting the
God within us take charge. Occultism is not simply a mental system; it is a training for life, for real life, for the life of the ages, and
not just for the life of one personality. It is not just for the life of the
world of two thousand years or so. It is a training for the life of
eternity; it goes on when everything else shall cease to be. As we
develop under the will and wisdom of the Eternal Spirit, we shall
still persist as spiritual beings going forth into new universes. That is
the goal, the end product of occultism.

Questions from the Floor and Answers

Question: I would like to know how you can recognize the truth. Surely our problem is that we cannot always recognize it—not until afterwards, that is.

W.E.B.: Looking for truth is rather like looking for the bottom of a well (where Heraclitus tells us it lies hidden). There are two kinds of truth. One is relative and the other absolute. We invariably make the mistake of trying to get at absolute truth right away. When you meet absolute truth, when you experience it, it has nothing to do with thought or emotion. Suddenly, within yourself, it arises and you know intuitively and infallibly that it is the truth. It cannot be anything but the truth. But, for every occasion that you know something with certainty, you will have ten thousand experiences when you have to rely on indirect truth. Then you have to reason it through from cause to effect. You have to try to understand various laws and accept that, when you don't know all the facts or you don't know all the laws, relative truth can sometimes be distorted. You have to hold relative truth lightly. Most of what I've been telling you comes under the heading of relative truth. I may have been misinterpreting it. I may have given you a false emphasis. You have to start using your reason, asking yourself, "Is the old boy telling us the truth or is it a lot of nonsense?" You must all ask that for yourselves. No one can do it for you; you have to do your own reasoning. If you always rely on the reasoning of other people, ultimately you won't be thinking at all; you'll automatically be opening the door to let each last dispatch from somebody else come in. But, if you continue to meditate properly, reaching down to the Buddhic principle within you, the Divine within you, you will come to the truth. When that happens, you don't think it; you don't just realize it. You know it. No one can take that truth away from you.

Someone once asked Jung if he believed in God. He replied, "No, I don't believe in God; I know." I've given that same answer many times. When asked if I believed in life after death, I say, "I don't believe, I know." And that was long before I started reading Jung. As Browning said, "Truth is within ourselves."[2] If you can tear away some of the wrappings you've swathed around her, you'll find truth there. She is always there and always will be. Never worry about getting a relative truth which may turn out to be wrong. That's all part of the learning process. After a time, you learn not to accept without a good deal of reasoning and careful thought. It is all a question of relative and absolute truth. We rarely think with absolute truth. Until we've travelled a long way along the path, we will not be able to bring through that higher, deeper noesis which does not need to reason.

Question: Can you get the truth without meditation?

W.E.B.: You can. Sometimes it forces itself upon you. Meditation is a technique. You can indulge in a lot of meditation without knowing you're meditating. For instance, you walk through the woods to the river; and as you walk, certain ideas travel through your mind—and quite suddenly—the answer to your problem comes. Eureka, just like that.

Question: So you don't actually have to think?

W.E.B.: You haven't been thinking at all. Meditation is a technique in itself, but not an end unto itself. You can meditate absolutely anywhere, indoors or out. You don't have to sit in a lotus position or invoke various gods and goddesses. Meditation is a simple technique which I can teach you in a quarter of an hour. But once you get started on that technique, there are all kinds of subsidiary aids—things which you can use to improve the quality of your meditation. In that lies the whole science of meditation, for there is a science to it. Meditation in itself is a natural human faculty; and once you open yourself to that idea, you will find you can meditate on top of a bus or in the middle of Piccadilly Circus. My first teacher told me that if I couldn't meditate in a busy street or railway station, I was no good at meditation. Even with noise and bustle going on around you, it is still possible to retreat into the silence. Certain aids are helpful in the beginning, but they are only crutches, so to speak. Ultimately you learn to use the mind in a certain way and then the crutches can go. You can meditate, contemplate. You can even have the Divine Union without any form of symbolism whatsoever. Of course, and you must remember this, just as you reach up to the Divine, the Divine also reaches down to you.

A few years ago we had a bereavement in our family—a little girl, my granddaughter—and it hit me pretty hard. I knew the child lived on. I knew this physically because I had seen her after death. But her death had affected my daughter, her mother, very badly; and some of that misery had rubbed off on me. At that particular time, I was walking along a Southampton street, feeling absolutely wretched and depressed. I certainly wasn't reaching up to the Divine; but as I lifted one foot to take a further step, someone stood in my way. It was power, love, and wisdom. I was enfolded in the arms of that being; and while he held me, all the bitterness and sorrow drained away from me. I was lifted up, taken out of my misery. In the next second, my foot came down on the pavement and I was walking on. In that fraction of a second, the Eternal, through one of His sons, had manifested in me. I hadn't asked for it, and I hadn't expected it. There are many people who have gone through worse suffering and never experienced anything like that; but by the random operation of some law, it came to me. If anyone asks of me—"Who do you think the Christ is, an ordinary man or what?"—I can only answer in terms of my own experience. When I came in contact with that being, I knew that the Divine Self was shining out from that man. I would have gone on my knees before Him, for through that man shone forth my Lord and my God. It was a pure mystical experience which came and went in that fraction of a second.

Hundreds of people have had similar experiences. They come like the wind and list where they will, not where you would like or expect. They demonstrate that beyond all phenomenal things the heart of the Eternal is most wonderfully kind. Whatever we may think to the contrary, we are in a friendly universe. Let me give you a passage which comes from St. Paul (I love that man. A whole lot of people don't like him; they say he is an anti-feminist.):

For I am persuaded, that neither death, nor life, nor angels, nor
principalities, nor powers, nor things present, nor things to come,
Not height, nor depth, nor any other creature, shall be able to
separate us from the love of God, which is in Christ Jesus our
Lord.[3]

The Eternal Love cannot be separated from us. Always the Eter-
nal Hound of Heaven chases us down the days and down the nights
because we are of His nature and ultimately He catches up with us.
We fight; we flee from Him; but finally that love takes us up into
Himself, for that is the end of all manifestation. We return to the
Eternal from Whom we came.

THE
WITHDRAWN ORDER

The title for this talk is "The Withdrawn Order." Because several of you have asked me about it, I feel it is better to discuss it rather than let you go away with a glamorized version of it. In the normal course of events, it isn't something you hear much about. It's seldom talked about, and yet its work is of the utmost importance to the occult scene.

We've been discussing fraternities, groups, and brotherhoods, all of which exist on the physical plane. They are all working in their various ways in the East and in the West, whether they are of "the Andes or of the Ganges," as the old Rosicrucian saying goes. They are all more or less separate organizations; sometimes they are linked together by the chiefs of the individual orders, but the orders themselves remain separate. That is a good thing in many ways because no two people are the same. The different orders and groups cater to different mentalities and different outlooks, to different races and different ideas. If they are doing the work properly, these various orders and fraternities are contributing to the spiritual evolution of mankind. That is their purpose, their job, and the reason for their existence. Still they are not the only pebbles on the beach.

The head of every effectual group or fraternity is "contacted," as we say. That means he or she is in a telepathic, psychic link with others who are behind the scenes on the inner planes. An invisible group of people of like mind on the inner plane is linked to every contacted group here on the physical level. The group above beams in, so to speak, on the meetings and rituals of the physical group and links telepathically with it. Behind the inner plane group are the inner plane teachers or masters. Each of the teachers has a number of groups of the same school under his or her jurisdiction, that is, of the same tradition or culture (for example, the Egyptian tradition or the Rose Cross). The invisible group then makes telepathic contact with the teacher or leader of the group on the physical plane. If that leader keeps to the ideals which he or she has set out for him or herself and the group, if the group runs along harmonious and correct lines—in other words, does as it is told and doesn't try to bust things up—the leader of the contacted group will receive real inspiration through this contact with the inner plane. Those on the inner planes will pass through to the outer plane all the teaching that is necessary.

That is the way in which groups are organized, but each group in itself also acts as a kind of greenhouse, a forcing house for the supernormal faculties of its members, a place that enables members to make their own contact. First of all, the leader must make his or her inner plane contact because upon that depends whether the leader has the power to initiate others. If the head of the group hasn't that contact and the power that comes with it, he or she is unable to initiate others into the mysteries. As you know, when you see it in action, this telepathic power from the unseen is a very real thing, indeed, almost tangible at times.

The leader once having received that power must make the best use of it and can do this by training himself or herself and the group to prepare and set up the best conditions through which inspiration may be given. Properly trained orders and fraternities will fast from meat and alcohol before entering their hall or temple for work or ritual. They have a bath to ensure that they are scrupulously clean and they wear different clothing. It's all a part of getting conditions just right, as near perfect as they can manage. They have to prepare themselves physically and mentally, and they have to adjust their minds to the telepathic power pouring in on them. Unless that preparation is carried out beforehand, you shut down the power just as if you had turned off a switch because that sort of power needs a pure and clear channel through which to flow.

Purity is important, but purity in the occult sense isn't a matter of sex or anything of that nature. It means one-pointedness, one thing only. An element is pure only when it is on its own, unadulterated. If you add another element to it, it immediately becomes impure. That is why chemists talk about impure salts. They don't mean that rubbish has been added, but simply that it is impure in the sense that another substance has been added to it. So people joining or being initiated into a properly contacted group have to prepare themselves and to understand quite clearly that the results they get will depend largely upon their own approach. Those on the inner planes do their best, but unless they are given the right conditions, they can't give their full support and teaching.

Tennyson interprets it very neatly in a poem:

> How pure at heart and sound in head,
> With what divine affections bold
> Should be the man whose thought would hold
> An hour's communion with the dead.

He goes on to say how "the dead" stand at the gates and hear the household jar within, and because the household is jarring, they can't get through:

> But when the heart is full of din,
> And doubt beside the portal waits,
> They can but listen at the gates,
> And hear the household jar within.[1]

It is the same for the teachers on the other side. They cannot come through to help their group unless the group does its part in creating the right conditions for them to do so. That means that every single member of the group has to take himself in hand in order to get the best results.

At one time I belonged to such a group, a strict, well-run organization. I used to bicycle no mean distance from Weybridge to Wimbledon to get to this group's meetings. At a quarter to seven, the doors of the hall were closed and locked. I arrived on several occasions at one or two minutes past the quarter and found the doors shut against me. Wearily, I got on my iron steed and pedalled back to Weybridge. It was no use banging on the door. I would never have gotten in. I was late and, therefore, no entry.

The same ruling applies to the Society of the Inner Light. You have to be there on time. Otherwise the doors are locked, and you're on the outside looking in. I've done that more than once, arrived a little too late, and had to sit outside the lodge room and wait for them to finish. At the time, I used to take it very hard because I had often come all the way from Southampton to London to go to a particular lodge meeting. I had only to miss a tube train or for that train to be late (which happened fairly frequently) to arrive late. It wasn't my fault; but that was the rule, and rightly so. I believe it still holds good today. We had to be there on time, clean, and spruce—washed behind the ears and all the rest of it. We had to arrive calm and unexcited. If we were steamed up through having to rush to get there on time, we were given a quarter of an hour's grace in which to meditate and calm the mind, to get our breath, so to speak. Then the meeting started, and I don't think I've ever seen more genuine spiritual phenomena—not all that astral stuff, but real spiritual phenomena—than I saw in that particular group.

The group was run on stern, austere lines. They made no allowance for any weakness on your part. If you weren't there, you were out until the next meeting. After a while, you developed a sense of self-preservation which made you get there on time because it was worth going and you were willing to pay the price in energy and foresight to make sure you did get there. In all the orders where there is any kind of discipline at all, that rule is applied. I belong to two fraternities or orders (one's the Inner Light); and they both stress the same thing: You must obey the conditions. And we're training the inner order of Ibis Fraternity with the same strict discipline.

It is the same with all the real fraternities because they are engaged in a delicate psychic operation, linking people together, making conditions such that they can bring through teachings that are better than average. Because of that, the heads of groups cannot afford to have anyone arriving at any old time, or mixing their contacts, or anything of that nature.

As I said before, the orders vary. Some follow one particular teacher, some another. Some are linked with the Egyptian tradition and get their power through a contact with that tradition; others bring through their power from a contact with the Rose Cross tradition. Those traditions exist on the other side in the astral worlds. Each teacher on the outer plane gathers together his own special type of people, who by their temperament, are drawn towards the group.

The outer plane group is no use unless it is reinforced by the people and power of the inner planes. This also applies to many do-it-yourself occultists. Say someone decides he is going to study the mysteries or has the urge to start a discussion group. He hasn't very much knowledge; nevertheless, he determines to have a go at it. If he does this with sincerity and intention and perseverance, sooner or later he will attract someone on the other side who is interested in what he is doing, and a tentative contact is made. He begins to understand principles and to apply those principles in practice. He forges ahead; he perseveres and finally makes a contact, a genuine inner plane contact. Then he begins to receive his teaching intuitively, but he still has to learn to keep the channels pure.

But all these organizations are separate. Each lodge works according to its particular ideals, according to the ideas of its founder or the person who is running it at the time; and they can differ considerably. In any case, the Withdrawn Order overshadows all of this.

You may learn and hear about an order like the Golden Dawn, but you won't hear anything about the Withdrawn Order. No one writes about it. With possible exceptions, no one speaks about it. No one acknowledges being a member; and, as far as the average person is concerned, it might as well not exist. However, it is a definite order of men and women, occultists and initiates of the highest degree who form a group which overshadows all other groups. It is the parent group behind the lot; and that parent group consists of souls of all nationalities, east, west, north, and south. In the West it works by the methods of the West, and it operates through the various lodges and groups. That Withdrawn Order is never named; no one knows its name because it has never been given one that we could understand. Actually the name is a combination of sounds which are not phonetically pronounceable, like the Gematrian names that interpret different number values but are not names in the ordinary sense.

The Withdrawn Order remains nameless because it doesn't allow itself to come out into the open. It inspires; it guides; it energizes the lesser orders. It is not necessary that it should come out into the world, not necessary that it should do things in full public view. That is the responsibility of the discussion circles and do-it-yourself groups. That is their work. The possibilities are shown to them by the nameless order, which then leaves them to get on with it.

The Withdrawn Order has the principles. It has the plans and it has the power. When the contacted orders come to it, they become recipients of those plans and power. It is an enabling, energizing, sustaining, and satisfying background to all white occultism.

The occult is a queer field. It's cluttered with all kinds of charlatans and all manner of nonsense, frauds, and imposters; but that's only the froth on top. Beneath all that superficiality is the real thing, sound as a bell, unbothered by all the bits and pieces floating on top.

The nameless order exists so that the will of God may be done in the world. It draws unto itself only those souls sufficiently evolved to be an asset to its work. No one can gatecrash; there's no place there for the joiners. (A joiner is someone who likes to belong to six or more groups at a time. This is useless, really, because he's squandering energy and possibly money over six different fields of activity. The result is he doesn't do any real work for any of them and can't justify his existence among them—as he might if he devoted his energies to one, or at the most, two.)

Unless you work without any kind of personal prejudice, you will not be able to come into contact with the Withdrawn Order or to draw power from it. Nevertheless, although you may not be able to contact its members, they can always make contact with you. It is an order without ceremonial trappings, and there is no way you can recognize the people who belong to it.

There are many individuals as well as groups taught by the Withdrawn Order. Someone shows himself willing to teach you, someone you know who has what it takes to be a teacher. When this happens and you accept, more often than not this means you have made contact through that someone with one or more members of that nameless order. When that contact is made, you get a curious, virile power coming down to you. It is by no means imaginary and seems to come from a great height. You get the impression that those behind that power are endowed with a wisdom beyond our knowing. You sense the love they have for you and for all mankind. And you sense, too, the will that carries them through. This will makes them the guiding spirit of the other do-it-yourself organizations which depend on material construction and administration.

The Withdrawn Order exists in its own right. You've come, as St. Paul said, "to the spirits of just men made perfect."[2] They are the watchers, the holy ones, men and women to whom this universe owes nothing. They know they participate in the whole life of the universe, and they understand it intuitively. They are those souls who have conquered life—not beaten it down—but conquered it. They are free to do their work in a way that an ordinary member of a lodge cannot. They are free to choose where to send their influence and free to choose where to stop sending it. They are free to help a particular person. They have no rules as such. Their rules are the rules that are written in their hearts. They know the law because it is part of them.

Those followers or disciples of the Withdrawn Order stand behind the lodges and fraternities on the physical plane—trying to help them, trying to guide their spiritual leader. They come quickly to assist if the lodge is in difficulties, but they never announce their presence. And, as a rule, those who know of them keep their mouths shut. I'm the biggest fool in that way. I keep opening my mouth; but although I can tell you of their existence and their work, I cannot tell you where they stem from or anything else about them.

They are the Withdrawn Order by their own choice; it's not because they are selfish or wish to limit their power to help others. They help humanity in a unique way, and that way involves being withdrawn from the ordinary phenomenal aspect of matter. They work from an entirely different angle, but it's just as efficient in the end. If you are ever in trouble, in sickness, or in need, or have any other disability and are desperate for help, you can always call upon them; and they won't refuse. Naturally you are expected to have a go on your own account first; but if you cannot resolve your problem, it's quite legitimate to ask help of the Withdrawn Order. They are not bothered whether you're first degree, second degree, or fifty-second degree. All that concerns them is that they do the will of God. You could say they are the will of God made manifest in human form. The will of God takes place around them. They are true catalysts in the spiritual order. They are the watchers, the backbone of all occultism.

The Withdrawn Order is the real power behind the occult scene. Its initiates and adepts go out into the world. There is no place they do not go. They are not bound by geographical limitations. East and west, north and south, are meaningless to them because wherever there is a need of their help, they will be found. They have many groups in existence. One of their members makes telepathic contact with someone who is keen to make reforms, or something like that. He makes contact with that person who then gathers around him others of like mind. And, under the right conditions, those of this unseen order, working telepathically, will bring those people into the invisible lodge.

We have all these separate little lodges. But the different lodges are not superfluous because different lodges deal with different aspects of occultism. Some of the lodges become teaching schools, where the spirits of those people who are able to travel out of the body in the sleep state are drawn and are taught and are instructed. Or there may be a place where a master or teacher concentrates his teaching and forms an ashram. Then it is a master's home, where he lives and works. An ashram doesn't exist only on the inner planes; it also manifests on the outer plane.

The great inner order above depends upon the Withdrawn Order. (Bear in mind there are orders within orders as you go up the planes.) The Withdrawn Order is the intermediary between those greater orders and the lesser ones down here. It's a great hierarchic

chain, starting at the top and working right down. It's been described as Jacob's Ladder—the angels walk up and down thereon.
Another name is the Tree of Life—again with the angels walking
up and down its branches. However you describe it, the principle
is the same. The Withdrawn Order is comprised of individuals who,
as nearly as possible, are the lenses through which the love of God
shines forth and His power is made manifest. There is never a time
when the members of this nameless order are not working in the
land, working amongst us. They are closer than hands and feet,
because they have the unique power to descend to the lower levels
of the material world in a way very few others have.

Working here in the material world, they are able to give to
people, through initiation, an inspiration that will lift them up. As
the Christ said, "And I, if I be lifted up from the earth, will draw all
men unto me."[3] That's true enough because we are all roped together in a mighty chain, climbing the mountain, linked together.
That chain is each one of us and we ascend to heaven in a serpent-
like manner. Again, as it is written, "And as Moses lifted up the
serpent in the wilderness, even so must the Son of man be lifted
up."[4] And so shall all the sons and daughters of man be lifted up.

The Withdrawn Order sees to it that there are always recruits
ready for training for entry into its ranks. It scours the world and
selects those whom it thinks ready and malleable (a person might
be ready, but not always trainable). The Withdrawn Order brings
those they have chosen into contact with the ashram, the center
where the master is working.

Now, the choice of an ashram, the choice of a teacher, is very
important. If you want to be patted on the head every time you do
some little thing right, choose a teacher who is very benevolent.
There's a snag to that, however, because there comes a time when
that teacher's training stops short of the ideal and you find there's
something within you which hasn't been eradicated through that
teaching—some little black spot within yourself which you cannot
seem to erase. It's rooted there in your personality, and it's very
reluctant to leave.

In its working, the Withdrawn Order approaches very close to
every student of the mysteries. There is no individual who doesn't

have or hasn't had contact with that order at some time or another. You can't brag about it because they never tell you anything, but they are there all the same—showing you the way telepathically, getting you out of scrapes, or whatever. You never realize what's going on; still, in some queer sort of way, things happen. They happen because the Withdrawn Order has seen to it that they do happen.

Some of you were asking me about the occult police. There's a particular branch of the occult police known as the Hunting Lodge, which is based upon the Withdrawn Order. The hunting lodges work to counteract the misuse of psychic powers, and they are manned by those who stand in the background as part of the Withdrawn Order. If you're ever in real trouble and need to clear evil, you can always use the sign of the hunting lodges and they will come to your aid. But, in the first place, you have to do part of the work yourself; otherwise, you get nowhere. If you do your bit, they will do the rest.

This Withdrawn Order—the Watchers, the Holy Ones—are always there in the background. Once you are in touch with them, whether it is directly or through the group to which you belong, you can be sure of this: You may be tempted; you may be tried, even temporarily overwhelmed; but you will never be overcome. Through all the storms and vicissitudes of life, there will always be help at hand. That's one of the great things about this particular school. There are those around us whom we do not see, and yet they are far more powerful than those we do see. Their influence and their power can come through to help us and our brethren.

There is no law against helping ourselves, to seeing to it that we have the conditions whereby we can do good for others. If you've nothing in the larder at home, you can't go out and feed the needy. And so it comes back to that unseen order. They supervise the whole of occultism, every aspect of it—even that aspect of the occult arts which forms a grey magic of its own. Every application of that grey magic is met by a counteracting magic in the self, and that counteracting action is initiated by those dwellers of whom we have been speaking. They are the true masters of life behind the scenes.

Don't forget! The higher the master is, the nearer he is to you.

Don't accept the idea of masters being remote and far away. As Madame Blavatsky said about hers, "They have taken away my masters and made them into stars, but I tell you they are living human beings." She was quite hurt about it. People had idolized the masters to such an extent that the picture had become glamorized.

As human beings, they have come through all the experiences which we have gone through—in other civilizations, in other lives— and now they stand where they go out no more. They stand on the inner planes as focus points, as lenses which may trap and concentrate the rays of the supernal, spiritual sun upon those who have need. That power coming through is the real power of the Absolute working in that way, brought through to those who have need. That work is done by the unknown withdrawn brethren. They are there to minister to you, if you'll let them. They are initiates inspired by those Lords of Light who belong to the higher grades of occultism. They send out their light and life into the world in a kind of torrent which sometimes overwhelms you. Some people receive nothing because they are looking in the wrong direction. But, for those who look in the right direction, the withdrawn ones come near to them. We're never really alone, and even less alone when we think we are alone:

> *But there are moments which he calls his own,*
> *Then, never less alone than when alone,*
> *Those whom he loved so long and sees no more,*
> *Loved and still loves—not dead—but gone before,*
> *He gathers round him.*[5]

Those of the Withdrawn Order are living, spiritual beings— perfected in this phase of evolution—who come as close to us as hands and feet, as close as breathing. They come to inspire and to help, to train and to lead. They work in the shadow of our personalities to bring light where there is darkness, joy where there is sorrow, and peace where there is strife. The Withdrawn Order doesn't advertise its existence. It is sufficient for you to know it is there and will come to your aid when called upon. But you must be prepared to help yourself first before the withdrawn ones can approach you; then they can work miracles on your behalf. But, remember, no spirit, however great, has the right or the power to invade your personality unless you let it in. That's the key. You can open the door to undesirable things; you can also open the door to the beautiful and the true. Whichever way you go will determine your future. But I know this, there is no more joyous or happy service in the universe than being a servant in the service of the holy ones of the Withdrawn Order.

As we sit here tonight, there are those of that order among us. And there are those among you in need of help, deep interior help, who are already getting it. This help is being sent telepathically to you from those people who stand by your side and are giving you something of their power, their love, and their wisdom. Remember, they are of our company—the company of humanity—but are not of our earthly company. They are here to bless and to lift us into the higher realms of light, truth, knowledge, and peace. Nothing is done in a spectacular fashion, but it is done efficiently. There's no wasted energy. Then they depend on us. Once that fertilizing stream of inner knowledge has come into our minds, what we have to do—must do—is not just to say thank you and hop off, but to say thank you and then go and serve. We take the power that is given to us and use it to help other people; and, in doing that, we also help ourselves.

We give, but we also receive. That's the key to the whole of life. There is the other side to giving: If nobody were willing to receive, you couldn't give. Blessed are they that receive as well as those that give. Sometimes we think it's beneath our dignity to take something from another, but that isn't so. There is that reciprocal action: By receiving, we enable someone else to give. And, if we give love, we never lose it. It's part of ourselves, bound round our hearts like an amulet of security. If you lose your life in helping others, in working for others, you'll find it because the small personal life is taken up into the great cosmic life. You will love with the love of God, which is not the emotional kind that we think of as love.

In that great cosmic life, the unseen Withdrawn Order loves

humanity with a love so great that we cannot understand it. It loves humanity, however sinful it may be. It hates the sin but loves the sinner with an all-embracing love—with the love of the Absolute, which the unseen order brings through each of its members.

Now I know that the unseen order exists, and you can know it if it ever comes your way. But you have to be working in the path of light before it can approach you. When that happens, you suddenly feel sustained by some influence which flows in to you and stirs you to activity in the light. When that happens, be happy and know it may come from that august fraternity of the Withdrawn Order. We are none of us so bad it cannot reach us, and none of us so good that we deserve to be reached. Yet, always, it stands in the background waiting to serve and to bless.

That's all I can tell you about it. It's all I should tell you about it. I want you to realize that we are in a friendly universe. In the end, there is no room in the universe for anything but love. It's love that makes the world go round. Dante refers to that same love in his "Paradiso":

> *In even motion, by the love impell'd,*
> *That moves the sun in Heaven and all the stars.*[6]

In that same work, Dante describes meeting some very happy and contented people. And it seems to Dante that they should be striving towards something better. After all, they're not down in hell, nor are they up in paradise. They are in an intermediate position (the first heaven), and he doesn't see what they have to be so happy about. He asks them why they are so happy and why they are content to stay as they are and not get any higher. Have they no will power? They answer, "In his will is our peace."[7]

And that's a nice little motto to carry away with you: In the will of the Logos, in his will, is our peace. Peace, not a negative absence of warring factions, but a positive quality. Whatever society, group, or order we belong to or join as occultists, the aim of all is to do the will of the Absolute; and, in doing that, we shall find our peace, a true peace, the peace that passeth the understanding of mankind.

That is something which, in our hearts, we all yearn for and which we shall ultimately gain—whether it is now or later is another matter. If we start right away and say to ourselves, "I am going to tread the Path. I am going to be of service to humanity and of service to the Divine"—if we let no obstacle stand in our way, let nothing turn us aside, the time will come when we will know we have served God and mankind. We will have brought ourselves into a condition of light and love and happiness and peace which, at the present time, the mind of man cannot conceive.

WOVEN PACES
AND WAVING HANDS

The title of my subject—"Woven Paces and Waving Hands"—comes, as you probably know, from Merlin and Vivien in Lord Tennyson's *Idylls of the King*, wherein the witch Morgan le Faye, or Vivien, puts a spell on poor old Merlin. She works (against him) the magic he has taught her using the spell of "woven paces and waving hands," putting him into a trance. She then flees down the glade calling him a fool:

> *For Merlin, overtalk'd and overworn,*
> *Has yielded, told her all the charm, and slept.*
> *Then, in one moment, she put forth the charm*
> *Of woven paces and of waving hands,*
> *And in the hollow oak he lay as dead,*
> *And lost to life and use and name and fame.*
> *Then crying 'I have made his glory mine,'*
> *And shrieking out 'O fool!' the harlot leapt*
> *Adown the forest, and the thicket closed*
> *Behind her, and the forest echo'd 'fool.'* [1]

Yes, it was very foolish of the old man to let himself be caught that way. There's a lot of "woven paces and waving hands" in ceremonial magic. I've worn out a few pairs of slippers in my time treading magic circles. I've never spoken much in public about ceremonial magic. I never take part without knowing the exact intention of the ritual, what it is hoping to achieve. I also like to know a little about my would-be fellow ritualists, too.

Never enter into a ritual just for fun, for kicks to see what happens. You can upset the whole works, upset both yourself and those taking part with you. The magic circle is not valid unless you yourself believe in its efficacy to protect you. If you enter in the spirit of the dying atheist who prayed—"O Lord (if there is a Lord), save my soul (if I have a soul)"—you won't get very far. You will neutralize whatever it is you or your companions are trying to do. Yes, there are people like that. They get into a magic circle; they don't believe in it; and, because they don't, the whole operation becomes meaningless.

On the other hand, if our unbeliever gets into a magic circle with seasoned ritualists who know what they are doing and believe in it, then the psychic force or power (whatever you like to call it) will affect him, will affect even the most skeptical. However, a strong magic circle can't tolerate too many skeptics because they act as a blanket on the rest of the company.

Before we go any further, a word about "ritual" and "ceremonial" and the distinction between them. Ceremonial is a certain way of doing a thing whereas ritual is something that is done or acted out. Generally speaking, the two are more often than not employed together, and their separate meanings lost.

The basic point in ceremonial magic is psychological because you are appealing to the subconscious mind which works most effectively with pictures and images. This is because the subconscious mind was developed at a time when spoken language had not been invented. It is a pictorial language, which is why you can impress children (and adults, too, for that matter) with pictures more than with words. If those subconscious pictures or images are vivid, they have an immediate effect. That is one of the reasons we wear gorgeous vestments and work with symbols. In "The Power House,"[2] Dion Fortune describes a lovely robe worn by Dr. Taverner. It was stiff with embroidery and so heavy with bullion that it looked like the mines of Ophir. The vestment was so heavy that he couldn't raise his arms to don the headdress, and she had to do it for him.

Vestments have a psychological effect upon the person wearing them. You take off your jeans or working clothes, and you robe in

a vestment which carries a different association of ideas entirely.
You cloak yourself in a different personality, in your magical personality. When I am vesting prior to celebrating the mass, each
particular piece I put on has an appropriate little prayer to go with
it. I am mentally taking steps one after the other. Each piece of
vestment has a definite meaning for me as it has for all my fellow
priests in the Liberal Catholic Church. Because of that vesting ritual,
when I am clothed in those robes, they will speak to my subconscious mind. In the same way a girl, who is fed up with everything,
might go to her bedroom and doll herself up, put on a pretty dress,
and make up her face. This makes her feel better, but it's purely
psychological.

Our vestments have a definite psychological effect upon us, and
so does color. Color is intrinsically valuable in magical work as it is
in healing. Each color reflects a different symbolism or representa-
tion. For instance, if I were going to work a ritual in Hod, the
sephirah of knowledge, I would wear the orange-yellow of Hod;
and this would help me to keep my mind on my intention. Every
time I looked at my robe, automatically my subconscious mind
would think of knowledge, knowledge, knowledge. It would be
nudging me all the time. If I were working in Chesed and wearing
royal blue—or Netzach robed in emerald green—it would be the
same. Each time my eyes alighted on the color of the sephirah, it
would jog my subconscious mind to remember my intention. The
whole color system of qabalah, or the Tree of Life, is based on this
innate power of color to affect consciousness and evoke the appropriate response within the self.

Vestments also cut you off from the outside world in a curious
way. You feel you're on a different level. You have to experience
it to understand it. You're no longer Mr., Mrs., or Miss So-and-so.
You are, say, the *Dweller in the South*, "ruler of the Holy and Ancient Gate of Fire; from a time long past and a land now lost derive
you this office. . . ." You're sitting there in the seats of the mighty
in the South, and quite suddenly you feel isolated from the twentieth century. You're back there, in a time long past, but you are
impersonal. That is to say, you represent the long line of all those
who served at the altar of the Mysteries. The whole of ceremonial

is designed to make you feel different. Take incense, for example. That, too, has the power to alter your consciousness. You know how, if you smell a scent, your mind jumps back to when you first smelled that particular fragrance. You can see the people and conditions around you at that time. But, if you tried to remember back to that period consciously, you wouldn't have the same impromptu recall. Instead, the whiff of that scent brings it all back involuntarily.

That is why—in Oriental circles, in the Eastern Orthodox Church, the Roman Catholic Church, and in some Anglican Churches—they use incense. It is a symbol of fire and has a purifying effect; it also has a peculiar psychic value, an inner value, too. It affects your mind, your psyche. You can produce an atmosphere in a room very quickly with the burning of incense because those particles released in the smoke of the incense are charged. You get a similar atmosphere when you purify with water, but the water must first be blessed. Now blessing is the Christian equivalent of what we in occultism call "magnetizing" or "charging." Before you can charge your water, you must first cleanse it, free it from other influences. You end up with what is called "holy water," that is, water charged with energy.

Say I wanted to magnetize this pen for a writer friend to help him a little in his work. I would, first of all, take it so between my thumb and forefinger, and I should visualize a film of iridescent light running along the pen. I would then slowly make that light encircle the pen and interpenetrate it; and, as the light goes through the pen, it kicks out anything below its own vibration, demagnetizing it, making it sterile. But it must be done with intention. That's the vital point; it must be done with intention and an understanding of what the light is doing. After it has been neutralized, I can charge it with whatever quality I like. Because I want my writer friend to be a ready writer endowed with inspiration, I visualize vividly the image of one of the muses, say Calliope, to inspire wisdom in writing. But I could use any god form (Maat, Thoth, or Athene, the Greek Goddess of Wisdom) or any other figure or icon which represents for me the symbol of good writing. I pass my hand down the pen with that intention, and I impress my own psychic magnetism upon it. All the time I'm visualizing the chosen image, and the power has poured out from me into that pen, charging it with that particular image. Now, if the writer sits down in a receptive frame of mind, this pen will help him tremendously because it has been put telepathically and psychically in touch with the old archetypal forms behind the scenes.

That is how talismans and charms are prepared. If you buy a ready-made, ready-charged talisman, it will not have the same potency as if you had made it yourself or had a friend—who really knows how to make and charge a talisman—do it for you. Another thing: Never take money for charging a talisman. You can reclaim the cost of materials for making one (that's legitimate because gold or silver or whatever doesn't grow on trees just outside your house). But never charge money for magnetizing a talisman. Magnetizing has nothing to do with money; and if you start taking money for it, you'll lose your power.

Talismans or amulets can be useful because a charged symbol, when it is worn within the aura of the wearer, vibrates at a certain rate; that is to say, the mind of the person will be lifted up. That magnetizing has effected a small change of consciousness. It's a pure magical act.

But there is another aspect to it. That beautiful talisman you've made and charged for yourself is merely an aid, an extra bit of protection. You can't sit back and let it do all the work. You still have your part to do. You can't rely on it completely. There's a story about King Alfred, a legend really, and I suppose it has as much claim to truth as the legend of King Alfred burning the cakes. The king wore on his breast a beautiful jewelled talisman. One day, while riding into battle, one of his commanders said, "It's likely to be tough going today. I wish I had a talisman like yours to protect me." Alfred replied, "Only God can protect you," and to prove his point, he tore the jewel from his breast and threw it into the nearby marsh where it was found centuries later. That same talisman is now in the Ashmolean Museum at Oxford.

Never put your entire dependence on an inanimate or animate object or creature. You are meant to stand upon your own two spiritual feet, so hold your talisman in proper perspective. Then one day you'll find you no longer need talismans or symbols. You will be able to rely completely on the self within. It is the same with vestments. Once you reach a certain stage of development, you can manage without any of it. At that stage, it is all taken within you and becomes an attitude of mind. Then, at any time, in any place, you can exteriorize it around you. Your place of working has been immediately purified with water and fire; the psychic lines of force are produced by your own effort and will. You are no longer dependent upon collecting swords and wands, altars and lights. The power is inside you, and you can produce the same results without the ceremonial magic. But, until that great day comes, we make use of our props and our vestments because our minds are form builders, and symbols and images evoke the right response from within.

When you tread your magic circle in the lodge or temple and you are all walking solemnly in procession, psychic vision can actually see those lines of force formulating. It sometimes stops you in your tracks with this phenomenon. The curious thing is that although you're forming your magic circle on one level, you are actually building a sphere (those lines of force go, in equal distance, beneath as well as above). I once had visual proof of that.

I went to my lodge in the Inner Light after journeying from Guildford to London. I arrived a couple of minutes late to find the doors closed against me. It was no use my banging on the door. Not all the king's horses would have got me inside. Dion Fortune had a discipline and she kept to it. However, the library where one could sit and wait was below the lodge. I went there to nurse my disappointment. While I was sitting there relaxing after my journey, they started opening the lodge which was just above me. Suddenly I could see psychically that all around me was a circle of light. Upstairs where they were treading the circle was the center of the sphere, and I was seeing the lower half of that same sphere in the room below. I was in the lodge atmosphere, just as if I had been in the temple itself.

Don't forget that when you've formed your magic circle, you've formed a sphere of light, and you've trapped quite a lot of elementals within that sphere. They've come into your conditions, and they are helped by it. That magic circle, properly constructed, will keep out drifting thought forms. One of the problems in magical work is other people directing their thinking your way. Sometimes their thinking isn't very pleasant. They try to break down your defenses because they want to know what you are up to. Those who have the know-how are quite capable of sending nasty little thought forms your way, complete with horns and hoofs. But, invariably, if you look at the back, there's nothing there; they've visualized only the front appearance of the thought forms. They seldom visualize in three dimensions. The result is that all those beastly little thought forms are like papier-mâché. When you look at them properly, you can see there is no substance to them, and what is sent to frighten you becomes a little laughable.

But those who don't like you and perhaps have a grudge against you (and you can find that sort in occultism as well as anywhere else) will try to penetrate your circle; and, if they manage that, there is always the danger they may influence your thinking by their own mental images. That is one of the reasons why in a true lodge you don't divulge to anyone outside your group what it is you are doing. You don't tell them about your rites, or the times you work them, or what words you use, because that would give them entry into your circle with their thought forms. The whole of your sphere of working is a thought-constructed fortress in which you are going to manipulate thought forces, and you don't want extraneous forces coming in and getting in the way. If you had a beautiful piece of machinery running smoothly and perfectly, you wouldn't want an outsider to come along and pour an alien substance into its works. In the same way, you protect your psychic machinery from outside disturbances. If you tell outsiders what you are doing in the lodge, you weaken your defenses. There's no use in constructing a magic circle to protect you against drifting thought forms and forces if you open your mouth and tell every Tom, Dick, and Harry about it.

Modern occultists of the do-it-yourself variety often overlook something that the older type of trained occultist set much store by. What was greatly emphasized then, but seldom today, is the magnetic power of each individual. By "magnetic" I mean that a field of power streams out from each of us. Call it "magnetic"; call it "etheric"; call it what you will. We all have that power in the aura, and the aura doesn't stop it flowing out. As that power emanates from the aura, the aura itself expands; and we are linked with other people working in the lodge. Because of our common interest our auras mingle together. We build this composite atmosphere or power inside the magic circle, and it is in that magical atmosphere that the change of consciousness takes place that is the true magical work. Don't forget, magic is the art of changing consciousness at will. The group thought form, which is charged with the group power you have built up in the circle by your ceremonial, causes a change of consciousness in the group aura.

Everyone has a different type of aura, a different emanation. Some give out one kind of energy and some another. Some give out healing power. There are certain people who, when they go into a magical group such as we are talking about, remain completely unaffected by it. It isn't that they don't believe. The power simply has no effect on them; they don't feel any atmosphere at all. Ask them to write a report and they've nothing to report. The magic circle is a blank wall to them. Now here's the interesting part: When they are in the group, things happen. Take them away and half the energy disappears with them. They are catalysts or enzymes. They start the energies of other individuals working where otherwise they might not. Like the catalyst, they are not themselves affected; but, when they are among others in the circle, they have this energizing effect on everybody else. They're strange people, mostly redheads or auburn haired, and they seem to be endowed with this peculiar power of getting things moving. Completely opposite to them are the people with an equally peculiar power of stopping everything dead. Whether it is a magic circle or a seance room, the moment they put their nose through the door, everything falls flat. They kill the atmosphere stone dead.

Everything in that magic circle comes through you. You are the channel. There are people who think it is clever to evoke to visible appearance. But remember this: If you evoke a malignant elemental into a triangle of art, it has to come through you first; and that gives you nasty vibrations within yourself. Those who start playing around with what I call the darker side of magic—of evocation and calling up spirits from the "vast deep"—will inevitably deteriorate in character because they are bringing through their own psychic nature an elemental force which is not good and which will eventually affect them adversely. You can't have sewage running through a pipe without it leaving some dirt behind. So remember, anyone bringing through the lower elemental spirits is bringing them through himself. He is the channel. Collectively, they come through the individuals in the magical circle. What you see is the exteriorization of what is coming from within you.

In constructing symbolism for the circle, you usually have something which is appropriate to the job you are doing. But don't fall into the trap of thinking you must use a certain type of symbolism and never depart from it. In a qabalistic temple, the double cube altar is normally in the center, but other traditions may place it somewhere else—in the north, for instance. You can't tell someone he's wrong because he has his altar in the north or the south or wherever. It doesn't matter whether the altar is central or in one of the four quarters as long as it coincides with the particular dimension or tradition you have chosen for yourself. So you might say, "I've put my altar in the north because to me the north is the element of earth. It symbolizes stability and firmness, inertia; nothing moves from it. My altar will be in the north, and it shall be made of stone, heavy and inert."

So you put your altar in the north and you get the same results as someone who puts it in the center, or south, or east, or west. All these things are within you because it is as you make it. Like the Bellman in *The Hunting of the Snark* stated, "I have said thrice: what I tell you three times is true."[3] Magic is not a rigid orthodox formula, where if you alter one word, terrible things will happen to you. I know it is said in the Chaldean Oracles that you mustn't change the barbaric words of evocation, but that's for another reason (basically because they employ archaic names which mustn't be altered because they were associated with a particular system of magical ideas).

Never let yourself fall into superstition with regard to ceremonial magic and think that if everything isn't done exactly to someone's book, terrible things will happen to you. It's intention that counts. You can open and close a circle at will; and, if you do leave a tiny gap, no elemental is going to slip in and bite you—unless you think it is going to. Then you open up a possibility—a mere possibility, that's all. That circle will protect you even if it isn't properly closed. It is your idea of a closed circle that matters, not the fact that you missed the last inch when you went round with your wand or dagger.

Once you've learned the principles of ceremonial ritual working, you can build up your own. It's part of the training in the West. And, as you build up the rituals, you build power into them. And it becomes very potent because that particular form of ritual is individual to you. It isn't being spouted all over the country. Its power isn't diversified. You only leave unaltered the great rituals which we inherit from hundreds of thousands of years back because you are not in a position to monkey about with them.

When I'm working a ritual in the ordinary way, I'll build it up for myself to do a particular job (like I did with the pen). As a Liberal Catholic Priest, I could have done it more ceremonially. I could have demagnetized by quoting, "I exorcise thee creature of earth, by the Holy God, by the Omnipotent God, by Him Who filleth the whole earth with His majesty and glory; that thou be cleansed from all impurities in the name of Him Who is Lord alike of angels and of men."

That is a little exorcism which does the same thing and is equally effective, but I performed it in a different way. There again I could bless it in a similar way by saying, "Creature of earth, adore thy creator; in the name of the Eternal God I bless thee. . . ." These are two ways of doing the same thing—one ceremonially with charged water and incense; the other quite casually, as I did with the pen. Both ways are effective. As Kipling wrote, "There are nine and sixty ways of constructing tribal lays, And-every-single-one-of-them-is-right!"[4]

Don't get a blockage by thinking you must follow one particular book of words. You can save yourself money by not buying all those little goetic manuals, those textbooks of magical work. Take *The Sacred Magic of Abramelin the Mage.*[5] It is a wonderful little book, but you can boil a lot of it out and it will still be effective. Don't spend your money on various books of spells. Most of them are tripe, the kind of stuff they used to hawk at the back door to servant girls in the middle ages—love charms and potions, that kind of thing. So never spend your money buying expensive books on magic spells. On theurgy,[6] yes; read Iamblichus on the Mysteries[7] and you'll get something useful. Leave all that other hogwash alone. People who composed it had their tongues firmly in their cheeks.

The warden of a group I know compiles all their rituals herself, and very effective they are too. When she comes across a phrase or verse that impresses or inspires her with its image-provoking quality, she files it under a suitable heading so that when she comes to compile a ritual, she can draw from that file for the odd phrase or prayer. Because the scripts of those rituals are private and never leave the temple, there is never any problem of abusing copyright. In your private domain, you can read and copy what you like as long as you don't copy it for publication. As time goes by and you become more proficient, you can build on or amend your rituals; you can polish them to a high standard. And the beauty of it is that they are yours; no one else is using your formula of words in exactly that way.

You can build your ritual on the principles of the Tree of Life or whatever other system you are working on. Qabalah isn't the only tradition; there are other equally valid systems. There are both Western and Eastern traditions which don't depend on the Tree of Life at all. The principles behind the systems are the same, but the way in which they are worked is different. As long as you keep this idea firmly fixed in your mind, you can build your own rituals— using your own words or introducing little appropriate phrases from literature. Then, without fear, do it. As Edwards says in his little book, "Dare to make magic."[8] Know first of all, then will, dare, and keep silent. Keep your mouth shut about what happens!

Don't forget what I've said: Never harbor superstitious ideas about ritual; don't get hung up on the idea that you must wear a silk robe or you must wear a robe of a certain color—unless, that is, the rite you are working is going to be helped by that color. All your vestments and symbols are a means to an end—to exalt your consciousness. They have no intrinsic value; however, incense does get the magnetism working because of the dispersal of smoke. Water sprinkled round the lodge or temple has the same effect. Sprinkling with water and burning incense are very effective ways of charging a room with psychic force. And, of course, whatever incense is used should be associated in your mind with the work you are doing. If you read in a book that someone else burns a different incense (say for Jupiter) than the one you've been burning, don't get upset and panic. If you've already got a certain odor in your mind associated with Jupiter, stick to it. Remember, all ceremonial and ritual is an individual thing—except when you are working in a group, when you have to conform to that group's system and tradition.

One final thing. Sometimes it is a good idea to work a ritual just to say thank you to your god or gods. We all have much to be thankful for; and while we're being thankful, we should spare a few moments to remember all those less fortunate than ourselves. The little group I go to always concludes its rites with a prayer for all life and a special blessing on the animal kingdom. If you are lucky enough to have your own temple or even just a shrine in a cupboard, keep it scrupulously clean with daily attention. Some people keep a fresh flower on their altar or burn a light or candle daily because it means employing constant care and attention. You'd be surprised how that daily ritual of caring keeps the atmosphere charged.

It has been said that all ritual of the right-hand path, all prayers and invocations to the Light, help to raise the subconscious soul of humanity to the higher realities. When the consciousness of a group is raised telepathically, it becomes part of the cosmic dance. I leave you with these words, the promise of the neophyte at his or her initiation, "I desire to know in order that I may serve."

QUESTIONS
AND ANSWERS

Question: You have spoken about the responsibility of thought. Could you talk about the mechanics of thought? Are your thoughts what you observe or is thinking something you do?

W.E.B.: There are different opinions about this. It has been said by one authority that your thoughts are independent. You don't make them yourself; they spring up in your consciousness, as it were. Thought is a creative activity of the human mind and a quality inherent in humanity, and, to a lesser degree, in the animal kingdom. We make thought forms by the power of our thought and then we observe them in our consciousness. The thought form actually comes from the subconscious or subjective mind. We think, and the idea is accepted by the subconscious which sets it in motion in accordance with the strength of the emotion behind the thought. Say we're trying to remember where we've put something, like our glasses or a book. We visualize subconsciously the room where we think we may have lost that something. We create the thought form with that visualization and then, by consciously observing the thought form, we try to see whether it has any relevance to our present problem. It's a dual action all the time. You observe the thought forms, but you don't originate them in the conscious mind. That happens in the subconscious.

Question: How, then, can you be responsible for them?

W.E.B.: You're responsible for them the moment you receive them. You scan these thought forms with your conscious mind and then you can either accept them or banish them. That's your responsibility.

There are two methods of meditation where you use thought forms. In the first one, you allow the images to rise up from the subconscious without any input from your conscious mind. You just let them come up, take the lid off, and see what floats before you. In the other way, although it is actually your subjective mind that does the making, you deliberately create a thought form in your conscious mind. All you do with your conscious mind is simply give the command to the subconscious. I tell it I want a thought form of an orange and up comes an orange, but the engineering is all done down below. Whatever you are thinking, you don't create thought forms consciously at all. It's a very intricate mechanism which would take a couple of hours to explain in detail.

Briefly, the answer to your question is that thought forms are produced in your subconscious; they rise to the conscious mind, and it is the conscious mind's responsibility to accept or reject them. I can give you a simple, though potentially tragic, example. A mother watches her young child going off on his bicycle. He's going to cycle along a busy street for the first time, and she's filled with fear for him. Immediately the subconscious sends up a thought form of the child lying in the street in a bloody heap. Now the mother, if she knows anything at all, will expel that thought form double quick, slash it with a cross of rejection which the subconscious mind will understand. But, should she harbor that thought form and charge it with emotion by churning it over in her mind—well, it's simply asking for trouble. That particular thought form is created by fear, but it was the mother's responsibility to either reject it or dwell on it.

Question: I believe you said at one point that by means of magic one could lift the consciousness from one level to another. I've always understood that when that was accomplished, one could remain in complete control. Is there a borderline between that and the kind of advice we get from our higher selves?

W.E.B.: Yes there is. We can think of the personality as being a complete self-contained piece of machinery which is brooded over by the higher self, overshadowed by the higher self. Naturally speaking, it is like a piece of machinery that ticks along very nicely. It's a computer really, quietly doing its job. But, at a certain point, if what we call the "star of consciousness" is raised, we begin to be susceptible to what is coming through from the higher self. We would then experience what is known as illumination. Illumination is not dependent on the personality at all; it comes in from another source. The higher we send our star of consciousness—the higher we go—the nearer we get, metaphorically, to the higher self, and the more powerful are the influences which come in. If we meditate and we shift our consciousness to another level, we get a certain amount of illumination, though it may not be very much. But, when we keep on shifting consciousness, training ourselves to go deeper and deeper, or higher and higher, we bring ourselves more and more within the radius, the influence of the higher self; and we then begin to get illumination which doesn't depend on the lower mind at all. That illuminated influence coming in makes its own use of the lower mind images. For example, as light is reflected from an object, we see that object; in a similar way, light coming through from the higher self illuminates the ideas shaping in the lower mind, and those ideas take on a new significance. It's a question of what is called grades of significance; and, as consciousness is raised from one level to another, the significance of whatever is in the lower mind is altered.

It's a bit involved, but that's what happens. The person who shifts consciousness just for fun will get something; but if his mind is not organized, not trained, he will not get the same quality of illumination as somebody who has definitely organized his mind. The trained mind does the same when shifting consciousness, but the illumination coming through is more vivid because the ideas and concepts in his mind are more capable of reflecting the light of the higher self. So, although anyone can shift consciousness mechanically, not everyone has the ability to benefit from it.

Question: Would it be right to think that the magical part of it is not self-induced but is an incursion from without?

W.E.B.: This is where we come to the question of subjectivity and objectivity. I'd say the magical part is definitely from within. In magic, all the goddesses and gods, all the devils and demons, all the elementals and things that go bump in the night, which you evoke into a magic circle or invoke as a presence or influence—all come through yourself. For that reason, magic is something which affects the whole of the mind. The whole of the self is involved every time you partake in a magical rite, and definitely there is a change, a permanent change, in the consciousness of every person taking part because the magic of power comes through each one. That is why people who dabble with magic can often get themselves into a lot of trouble because they are upsetting the interior economy. Jesus said, "The kingdom of God is within,"[1] and so is the kingdom of hell. If you monkey about with the denizens down there, you're sure to get bitten.

Question: Could you say something about the rays—the green ray, the red ray, etc.

W.E.B.: Oh yes, a lot of nonsense is talked about the rays. You hear people say, "I'm this ray and that ray," bringing them down to the mundane level of newspaper sun-sign predictions. It's a convenient classification of course. The only trouble is that the interpretation varies from school to school. It's a philosophy that has been handed down from the ancient Mystery Teachings, and so different people have interpreted it in different ways. Every person and every animal incarnates under the influence of some ray or other. To go into the ray philosophy deeply would require several hours, and then we would only be scratching the surface. There's a lot of talk about the green ray and green ray magic. Dion Fortune devoted an entire lecture to it way back in the thirties. The green ray is the nature ray; it is concerned with the whole of nature and natural things. When I told you to go and sit with your back to a pine tree to recharge your batteries, that was a form of green ray magic. If you're trying to invoke the fairy forms, you're dealing in green ray magic; all the elemental kingdom belongs to this ray. According to Dion Fortune, the function of the subconscious comes under the green ray. We recover the methods of mental activity from the past through it.

Whatever ray we think ourselves as being, if we lose touch with the green ray, we lose contact with mother earth.

The other day, someone told me that I was on the purple-violet ray. After I thought about it for a while, I came to the conclusion that this was quite right, though I'd never heard myself described that way before.

There are seven rays all told, and they are said to control the centers or chakras of the body. They are red, orange, yellow, green, blue, indigo, and violet. But occult classification is very confusing because, apart from the green ray, different schools have different interpretations. You need a kind of rosetta stone to sort it out. I will give you a very brief classification as I know it myself and as it is related to color healing. The red ray, or first ray, is the power ray; it has been called "the great energizer" because it stimulates the nervous system. The orange ray, the second, is love-wisdom. The yellow ray, activity, stimulates the reasoning power and is said to be linked with the solar plexus. People on this ray have a compulsive urge for knowledge and still more knowledge. The fourth ray is that green ray we were talking about; it is harmony-balance. The fifth is blue, scientific, and at the same time linked with truth and spirituality. The sixth ray, indigo, is devotion, the ray of the Holy Ghost which is linked to the third eye. The seventh is violet; it is the esoteric ceremonial ray. The Great White Ray is the union of all the rays. You don't hear much about this; none of us can claim to come under the Great White Ray. It is the divine ray of the Absolute, the Christ Consciousness. Well, that's one interpretation, but there are others. In his book, *Esoteric Psychology*,[2] Dr. Baker interprets red as will and power; indigo as love-wisdom; green as active intelligence; yellow as harmony through conflict; orange as concrete knowledge; blue as devotion; and violet as ceremonial. If that hasn't confused you, well and truly, nothing will!

If you really want to go deeper into this philosophy of color and the rays, try and get hold of books by Roland Hunt[3] and Theo Gimbel,[4] though I cannot guarantee they will agree with one another. You have to make up your own mind about which system to adopt, and, once having decided, stick to it. Don't keep chopping and changing.

Question: That's the reason I asked, because there seems to be a certain amount of vagueness about it.

W.E.B.: Yes, there's too much vagueness, but a certain amount of vagueness is necessary; otherwise you get the wrong impression. For instance, look at it this way. If I would put an entirely new color scale on the Tree of Life (instead of red for Geburah, I replace it with blue; move red to Chesed, and so on—reversing all the colors of the different sephiroth on the Tree of Life), I should have to give all of these colors different attributes from their existing ones. For instance, red (which represented energy under Geburah), now in its new assignment to Chesed, would represent organization and benevolence. But, if I kept to my new color key on that tree and worked with it properly, I would get the same results as with the original Tree. The names and the particular descriptions of those names are secondary to the real purpose—the real purpose being a certain relationship in nature, in man, and in the universe. You get the relationship and you can portray it in any particular color you like—as long as you keep to the same classification all of the way through.

I expect you sometimes read books like Bill Gray's *Ladder of Lights,*[5] Israel Regardie's *Tree of Life,*[6] Dion Fortune's *Mystical Qabalah,*[7] or *The Kabbalah Unveiled*[8] by MacGregor Mathers? If you read more than one of them, you will find that one book says something quite different from the others. But, when you go back and study the other books and sort it out, you find it is just a matter of a different code. In reality, it means the same thing. Some people just love to mystify you. It's that "twopence colored" again; but when you're dealing in fact, I prefer "penny plain" myself!

Question: I've always understood with rays and their colors that, although you surround yourself with a color, it's not really a color but a vibration. It's just that color is easier to visualize.

W.E.B.: True in its way. Modern science confirms that light is due to intense etheric vibration. If you pass white light through a prism, you get a spectrum of seven colors, each with its own wavelength and rate of vibration. Color is a property of light, the wavelengths of which define the different colors. So, yes, color is a vibration. Because we can see color in all its beauty, it's easier to visualize than a vibration. Still, the same rule applies: Keep to your chosen color scale; don't mix the drinks! Whether you're working magic or doing a spot of healing, the color you choose is a key to the vibration. If you're visualizing yellow you set off the corresponding vibration within yourself. You are always applying that vibration as long as you are consistent and don't keep changing or amending your color scale. It's the intention that matters. If you're interested in color you could do worse than wade your way through Goethe's *Theory of Colours*.[9] There's also *Pure Colour* by Maria Schindler and Eleanor Merry.[10] The first part of this book explains Goethe's theory for you. There's a lovely little verse at the beginning of that book:

> *Sun, Cloud, and Rain beget the Bow.*
> *What moral there is calling?*
> *Look up. The Virgin-birth your eyes observe.*
> *God is the Sun, the Flesh is Cloud, the Ghost is water falling:*
> *Star-of-the-Sea is then the Rain-bow curve.*[11]

It's all there in the harmony of the rainbow.

Question: Regarding reincarnation: In past lives, would I have always been male or could I have been a woman?

W.E.B.: You could have been a woman many times. Depending on what your higher self is trying to achieve, you can still incarnate as a woman. There may be certain work you have to do that is better suited to a masculine body; alternatively, if it can be more profitably expressed in a feminine body, you'll incarnate as a woman. Then again you may have been unbalanced in the past—too much male and not enough female—so the personality is slanted towards the feminine side to balance things.

Dion Fortune once said she'd had a long run of female lives, but the life previous to this current one had been a real humdinger, a rip—roaring Spanish Main incarnation as a pirate. The nickname we had for her was the name of that Spanish Main pirate; and, when she really got going, you knew that pirate was there. You could see him in her.

When they recall past lives, a lot of people find they have had a number of male and female incarnations. I've been taught there's no particular rule. You can also incarnate with a group because you have formed certain karmic ties with that group—love-hate relationships which have to be worked out. But, if anyone tells you you must have four female incarnations for every four male incarnations and so on, he's talking rubbish. It depends entirely on the personality and the lessons it has to learn. One personality may learn in one lifetime what it takes another three or more lifetimes to learn. It isn't what we would like to do or be, but what is best for our development, the lessons we have to learn or experience. I don't normally talk much about past lives. I'm a little skeptical because I've met so many Julius Caesars, Cleopatras, and what–have–you; but I've never met an Egyptian dustman. Whatever you've done or left undone in the past, you will incarnate in the personality most suitable to redress some of the imbalance. The higher self will post you where there is the opportunity to work out your karma—your destiny, if you like. It doesn't matter how many times you incarnate as a man or a woman. What matters is that you achieve the required results.

As far as my own past lives are concerned, the last and most vividly remembered one was as a monk in Glastonbury; before that, a woman in Brittany; before that, a woman in Greece; and going further back, an Egyptian fallen on hard times; and an Egyptian male before that. You see what's happening. The first Egyptian was given responsibility and power and misused it; the second Egyptian paid off some of the suffering he had inflicted in the past, but didn't clear it all. The Greek woman continued to pay off a little more of the debt. The woman in Brittany, still suffering, was subservient to a brutal man who put the karmic record straight by giving her a taste of what she had handed out to other women in the past while in a male incarnation. The monk was a rest period. There may have been (probably were) other incarnations in between because it is the traumatic ones you tend to recall more than the uneventful lives. Or, of course, the very happy ones, like my Glastonbury incarnation.

There's no fixed rule. Whether you are in a male body or a female one depends on what you've been doing in the past, which lessons you need to learn, and how best you can learn them. It all depends on what the higher self is up to.

Question: Do you always advance when you reincarnate?

W.E.B.: No, unfortunately, you can regress.

Question: So you can keep bobbing up and down?

W.E.B.: Bobbing up and down? Yes, but you never go quite so far back as you were last time. It's a gradual progressing, sort of one step back and two steps forward. But there comes a time when you vow to yourself, "I would rather eat the husks the swine eat—to get my belly full, to live. What a damn fool I've been! Now I will return. I've left this place before and gone out into the wilderness and I've turned back afraid, but this time I'm determined to conquer." When that happens—when the personality says that and means it—the power from the higher self comes down like a flash of lightning, and you go forward. There is a school of thought that maintains that the number of incarnations a soul has to undergo is appreciably shortened by the study and knowledge of the Mysteries. In other words, the soul treading the path takes a short cut up the mountain.

Question: When you first begin as a human being, is it with a clean slate?

W.E.B.: Not quite a clean slate. There's a certain amount marked on it. The body of the animal kingdom is still with you and the particular outlook of the animal kingdom is imprinted on it. But, mentally speaking, yes, you have a clean slate.

Question: At that point, the beginning, do people actually choose the right path? Or do they automatically go over to evil and then have to make up for it?

W.E.B.: They dodge about from one side to the other because they are learning by experience. Evil doesn't exist in their philosophy. If they eat their grandmother, that's okay. Granny was ripe for eating, and they themselves expect to be eaten in due course. The spirit hasn't any real knowledge of the planes of life or the world of matter. It's what is called a "virgin spirit." It doesn't make contact with matter; it is instinctively aware of certain things outside itself, but any consciousness is dreaming away inside. The spirit remains in that state for a long time.

During Atlantean and Lemurian times, the spirit remained unaware on the physical plane, but acutely aware on the psychic planes—so much so that they didn't see the physical plane with the physical eye. They saw everything through their psychic sense. They were withdrawn. Eventually they had to be jolted out of that state. They lost that psychic ability and were thus compelled to make contact with the physical plane and learn its lessons. They had to learn to take control of the physical and emotional bodies; they had to learn to function in the concrete mind.

Question: Could you say if there is any specific teaching about vegetarianism, because there is a lot of controversy on the subject.

W.E.B.: There always has been, and doubtless the controversy will continue for many decades yet. Vegetarianism is a vexed question. Lao Tzu was vegetarian; Jesus wasn't, nor was Confucius. A lot depends on the conditions and teachings of the time. If you can be a vegetarian, that's great. It makes you feel good because you are not killing any form of life (of animal life, that is, because vegetables and minerals also have life; there is nothing dead in the whole universe). Nevertheless, from the point of view of individual development, it is very helpful to have a vegetarian body. But it isn't possible for everyone. I must have tried at least a dozen times to become vegetarian. I get so far; then my body begins to protest.* I've tried taking vitamins and trace elements so that I didn't need to eat meat, but every time, at a certain stage, my body kicked against it and I became ill. It's individual to the person, and if you can be vegetarian it's all to the good. It's a clean way of living and you get rid of

---

*Mr. Butler was diabetic and radical changes in his diet always tended to upset his system.

the muckiness of the slaughterhouses and the butcher's shops. If you ever saw the elementals hanging around a butcher's shop, you'd never eat meat again.

If your body won't accept vegetarianism—and there are many whose bodies won't—then eat sparingly of what is called the meat proteins; and, if you can, cut out red meat. After all we are, all of us, overfed with regard to the physical body. Half of what we eat is enough to keep our physical body working and fully charged.

Some people are vegans—that is, they don't consume any form of animal products at all—not cheese, not milk, not eggs. They eat only nuts, fruit, and vegetables.

When you come to think of it, our human digestive track is a modified fruit and nut digestive system. In the beginning, we didn't eat meat, only fruits and nuts. Our alimentary canal was designed to deal with those, but human evolution has modified our innards to enable us to eat meat. It's a case of teleological influence. We've become indoctrinated into becoming meat eaters because of the conditions of physical life on this planet. We've had to divert from nuts to meat; but, as we continue to evolve, there will come a time when we will revert back to vegetarianism. Then we shall have to modify our alimentary canal to deal with nuts and fruit again. Vegans try it, but many of those fall by the wayside because they are trying to bludgeon their innards to do something it is no longer equipped to do. To become a vegan, you must do it piecemeal, so to speak; you have to coax your innards to modify the digestive track, and not everyone's body is willing to cooperate.

If you can become vegetarian without ill effects to your health, then, as I said before, it's a very good thing on all levels. But, if your body won't accept it, don't try to force the issue by starving yourself. If, after repeated attempts, you find that a vegetarian diet upsets you, you are not helping yourself forward. Throw in the towel and admit to yourself that it cannot be done. If you believe strongly that vegetarianism is right, then affirm with a will that in the next life you will have the kind of body that will enable you to abstain from meat. Remember, these strong affirmations are carried over into the next personality.

Many people are of the vegetarian persuasion simply because

they don't like taking life, don't like killing. The truth of the matter is that you cannot destroy life; you destroy the animal body, but life goes on. It isn't the killing of an animal that is so wrong; it is the method of killing, the way of caring for animals that can be so wrong, even evil. You cannot kill anyone, your enemy, for instance, any more than he can kill you; you can only kick him out of his body. You come across this philosophy in the *Bhagavadgita,* "The Song of the Lord." Arjuna protests that he cannot kill his own friends and kinsfolk in the battle. Arjuna was of the warrior caste, but he refused when it came to destroying his own kind. Krishna, his charioteer, tells him that the men whom he would slay cannot be slain. The unreal has no existence; you cannot slay what is most real in a person. It slays not, nor is it slain. Further in the song, Krishna says that—like a man casting off his wornout clothes—the embodied one casts off its wornout body and takes on a new one.

Arjuna's mentor then says:

> If slain, thou wilt attain heaven, or if thou dost conquer, thou wilt enjoy the earth. Therefore arise, O son of Kunti, and be resolved in action.
> Hold pleasure and pain equal, gain and loss, victory and defeat; and therefore gird thyself for the fight.[12]

The spirit holds its garb lightly. Death isn't the ultimate evil and peril. We in the West think of death as something terrible, but it is just a matter of taking off an overcoat. Those of you who go out on astral projection have taken off your overcoats temporarily, and you know from your experience that death is meaningless. Nevertheless, that shouldn't prevent your being a vegetarian or a vegan if you feel it is right for you. Incidentally, all the vegetarians I have known have been exceptionally healthy people.

I don't want you to run away with the idea that I'm giving you license to go and kill your neighbor. Killing another human being is wrong by any standard, and the karma for it is heavy. War is the one exception. In this case, it's race karma, and we all take responsibility according to the degree of personal involvement and intention. It stands to reason that you cannot stand by and see your loved ones done to death without making an effort to protect them. But there we're getting away from vegetarianism.

We also have a responsibility to animals; and if we are going to accept their sacrifice (for that's what it is) by eating them, it behoves us to see they are well cared for and slaughtered without fear and without pain. To eat the flesh of an animal killed in fear doesn't do the psyche or the body any good either. The day will come when evolution reaches such a level of sensitivity that the killing and eating of our younger brethren, the animals, will be an anathema. But it will be a gradual progress.

In the ancient mysteries of Hermes, initiates were forbidden to eat meat, and their disciples and followers were exhorted to follow suit. They weren't allowed to eat of any dead thing or anything that had the gift of seeing. Sight was considered sacred. It was written:

> Purify your bodies, and eat no dead thing that has looked with living eyes upon the light of Heaven.
> For the eye is the symbol of brotherhood among you. Sight is the mystical sense.
> Let no man take the life of his brother to feed withal his own. But slay only such as are evil, in the name of the Lord.[13]

Anna Kingsford and her colleague Edward Maitland wrote an interesting book on the ethics of vegetarianism.[14] It's probably out of print now, but the authors go very deeply into the spiritual aspect of it. As a matter of fact, they refer to meateaters as making themselves tombs for the carcasses of animal corpses. Not a nice thought!

Question: Do you think that by recalling past lives you can get some perspective on the present life?

W.E.B.: Yes, and that's the only valid reason for doing so. Those people who go hunting through the Akashic Records to get an insight into their past lives to gratify their vanity—hoping to find they were Cleopatra or some powerful Egyptian priest—are doing it for the wrong reason. The only true motive for researching your past lives is that you may see the way you've come, how the past has affected the present, and why you have landed in your present lifestyle or even your present predicament. When you know that, you can project ahead and get some idea of your potential progress if you keep to your present path. Hindsight begets foresight, and that's the only reason why a person should be delving into the past. I don't go digging myself. The glimpses I've had of my past lives have come about involuntarily and have always pointed to a moral. It is said that when you are ready and when there is a need for you to know, then parts of your past lives are brought before your mental screen. For myself, I've enough aggravation dealing with this personal life without intentionally trying to bring through past lives.

Question: Isn't it true you can prompt some very unpleasant experiences?

W.E.B.: You can. I read of a case only the other day. A lady remembered her past life as a Cathar in the south of France during the Inquisition. They were doing their damnedest to destroy the whole Cathar religion. She remembered being burned alive at the stake and how strange she had found it that she should bleed when being burned. She saw herself bleeding, her blood sizzling in the hot flames. Would you like to open yourself to an experience like that? I know I wouldn't. You can find out about your past lives without that kind of horror. You can read the records, but that demands some intensive training which you don't ordinarily get. You hear people talk about reading the astral records, but that won't do you any good. You have to read a much higher record than that. The astral records are distorted with all sorts of material and thought forms which don't give you the true picture at all. The true records are much harder to get at.

Question: Is this déjà vu?

W.E.B.: Déjà vu is a curious thing. Most people think of it as a sense of having been there before, of having experienced a certain set of circumstances before. It's a form of paramnesia. This means that déjà vu isn't always what has gone before; it can be a preview of something yet to come in this life. At the present time, scientists are saying that one half of the brain is always a little ahead of the other, so that you see the future as though it is the present. That may be so in some cases, but not in others. If your spirit is of the Eternal, where there is no time at all, that spirit can flash through your mind a picture from the future. You precognize; there's no doubt that does happen. Some cases of déjà vu are just that: a person momentarily steps out of time and looks into the future. When we're talking about time and space, we're dealing with the Mysteries. We are using a coinage adapted to our peculiar way of thinking because, to our finite mind, we cannot really visualize something that hasn't happened. That is impossible. It hasn't happened, so how can one see it? And yet there are thousands of cases where it has happened.

I can give you one very interesting instance in which a man had images of a local funeral procession. He identified it as the funeral of a friend and he recognized himself as one of the bearers. In due course, the friend died; and the man, remembering his vision, vowed there was no way he was going to be a bearer. He wouldn't even go to the funeral. However, he felt he had to pay his respects to his old friend; so he watched the cortège approaching from what he thought was a safe distance. But, just as the procession reached him, one of the bearers fainted; and he found himself taking the place of the sick man and becoming a bearer. That seemed like fate to the man.

The mind of man has more powers than we realize. We are in a five-sense body and limited by our physical brain. Our consciousness doesn't let everything through; it screens a lot out, keeps it from reaching us. If all the vibrations and influences of the universe were allowed to impinge upon our consciousness, we would go mad. Our brain and our ordinary sense mechanism tone it down so that we don't get the full force of the impact.

Question: We hear a lot about hounds of defense, but what about cosmic cats?

W.E.B.: You can use any animal for defense. It's simply an astral form you build. If you think of a dog as defending you, that's okay. In ancient Egypt, they used cats as hunters. Because they used to hunt the wildfowl with their cats, quite possibly the Egyptians used a cat of defense. It depends entirely on your personal predilection. I build a dog of defense myself—an ancient Egyptian dog—because I rather like dogs!

Question: One very often sees written or hears in discussion a two-word phrase, "divine law," but one never hears it expanded or explained.

W.E.B.: Divine law, now how can I answer that one? Edwin Arnold's poem, *The Light of Asia,*[15] is a magnificent explanation of Divine Law. It's too long to quote here even if I could remember it, but it's a beautiful piece of work and worth studying. It's not difficult to find a second-hand copy; there have been numerous editions and reprints and many thousands of copies issued.

Divine law is roughly this: If we assume that the Eternal Spirit—whatever or whoever It might be—had a design in creating the universe, then it must be a meaningful universe, because He had reason for creating it. He wanted to do something in His consciousness, so He created the universe; and because it is created in His consciousness, it is stamped with the meaning that He has attributed to it. That meaning is implicit in every part of the universe—something which is urging, impelling things to strive towards the divine purpose, to fall in with the plan. That urge, that pressure, is behind all evolution, behind all life and all forms. It is the will of the Eternal which is the law of the Eternal, and it is the way by which the Eternal brings a scheme of His own into manifestation for His purpose. That scheme is the divine law working in every atom of the universe. It's not the kind of law that is written on tablets of stone and brought down from Mount Sinai. It is implanted in each and every thing. That same divine law is implanted in each one of us, and our efforts to seek perfection are really the pressure of God within us seeking for the perfection of His plan.

Stars sweep and question not. This is enough
That life and death and joy and woe abide;
And cause and sequence, and the course of time,
And Being's ceaseless tide,

Which, ever changing, runs, linked like a river
By ripples following ripples, fast or slow—
The same yet not the same—from far-off fountain
To where its waters flow

Into the seas. These, steaming to the Sun,
Give the lost wavelets back in cloudy fleece
To trickle down the hills, and glide again;
Having no pause or peace.[16]

No pause or peace because the Eternal is there behind it all, pressing his plan towards perfection. That is why the theologists tell you that you cannot do any good of yourself; the good that you do is done because God so wills it for you. You have, as it were, linked up with Him, so any good you do is actually God working through you. You are His instrument.

Before beginning, and without an end,
As space eternal and as surety sure,
Is fixed a Power divine which moves to God,
Only its laws endure. . . .[17]

"Only its laws," divine law. Dion Fortune once asked Dr. Moriarty how he would define God. He answered simply, "God is pressure"—pressure in the universe, impelling everything towards a certain point—that point being the manifestation of the fulfillment of the will of the Eternal. That is the divine law. As Edwin Arnold says, it cannot be turned aside by anything. You can't bribe it; you can't stay it; you can't sway it in any possible way. It simply goes on and on. It's impartial. It is part of the nature of God, and He cannot go against Himself. The Law is inflexible, and everything from the smallest electron to the greatest cosmos must work according to that law; and that is the greatest safeguard we have. Behind all things is the Eternal Will working for good through His law; and no matter what we do, His will will prevail and ultimately His purpose will be fulfilled. There may be temporary setbacks in His universe, but in the end the earth shall be filled with the knowledge of God. We can never be separated from the love of God, because that love is implicit in the whole universe and is implicit in ourselves, in our very nature as children of the Divine. The spark from that flame, that law, is written in our hearts and ever will be.

Question: How do we get ourselves separated from the divine part of ourselves?

W.E.B.: Because we fall into illusion. Our personalities are glamorized. We give false meanings to things; we interpret our surroundings wrongly because everything about us is illusion, is transitory, ever changing. Take a simple item like this glass of water. It appears real enough on the physical plane; but if we think about it—break it down to basics—water is composed of two gases, oxygen and hydrogen. They are combined to form water. They can be separated. The glass itself is made of silica and some other oxides. Silica can be reduced to an element, to its electrons, to the nucleus which lies beneath it; and it can be further reduced to three or four different levels until finally you arrive at something which is not matter at all. So actually I'm holding "no thing" in my hand which is "no hand." We live in this world of illusion; everything appears solid to our physical eyes. We take it for granted that this glass is impervious; but the glass will allow gases to get through under certain conditions, and small particles, mesons, can pass through without any trouble. X-rays go straight through it as does light. It is not impervious; it only appears so to us.

Our personality has become adapted to seeing this world in this particular way. But, looking at it from the point of view of the spirit, we are looking at a world of illusion. Nevertheless, it is this illusory world that has enabled us to evolve. In other words, we have evolved because of the illusion. It gives us ideas—ideas that are limited—and it is that limitation which supplies the friction that enables us to get a grip on things in a finite world. If we lived in a fourth dimension, we would know that nothing was solid, nothing closed up entirely. You'd simply be able to walk out of your immediate environment. There would be no question of being imprisoned; you could move in a fourth dimensional angle and walk right through it all because it is illusory. The fourth dimension transcends all physical dimensions of space. There are cases where people have entered that fourth dimension. Read Charles Fort's books.[18] He's written several books about oddities which have occurred, and which science refuses to acknowledge. There's the story of a farmer, his wife, and two children standing outside their house looking across the fields. Something the man saw caused him to go and investigate. He shouted back to his family what it was, something trivial, and began to walk back towards them. Suddenly he disappeared before their eyes and has never been seen since. Three witnesses saw him disappear in good light. Did he step into the fourth dimension?

Because we don't know yet what the limits are to this world of ours, reality may be far different from what we imagine it to be. Nevertheless, the things of this world are real enough after their kind. I don't think we can take that mantra of the theosophists too positively. It goes like this:

> *From the unreal, lead me to the Real*
> *From darkness lead me to Light*
> *From death lead me to Immortality.*[19]

"From the unreal, lead me to the real." We are never altogether in the unreal. We are always to some extent in reality, but we don't realize it. For the time being, the things we see on this plane in our everyday consciousness are real to us. We cannot say absolutely that they are nonexistent, because while it is existing, it is here. The teachings of qabalah put that very neatly. When we are working with our minds and brains along this line, we are using them in a way that was never intended. It is as though we are using a nutcracker to separate cream from milk. At the present stage of our evolution, our mind is not up to comprehending the fourth dimension, let alone infinity. We have to make the most of what we have and accept and work with our present limitations of time and space.

Question: Can you offer any helpful exercise for transferring consciousness away from the personality to the higher self?

W.E.B.: Yes, mainly through meditation. First you must give a good deal of thought and meditation to what the higher self means to you, what you understand by the term. Then try to evolve a symbol that represents all you know and imagine about the higher self. When that symbol of the higher self is clear in your mind (you might even make a physical symbol), sit down to your meditation with thoughts along these lines:

> I am not my higher self, my true self is elsewhere. I am only the personality. My personality is not my true self. My true self is different. My higher self will say of itself, "I am he that liveth and was dead and behold I am alive for evermore, and hold the keys of hell and death.[20]

The personality can't say that, but the true self can. You make a composite of all these thoughts and realizations into one symbol to represent the higher self; then you sit back and meditate upon it. By concentrating on that symbol, you begin to raise your consciousness towards the higher self, and gradually it begins to flow in upon you. It "flows through a wall," as my first teacher told me, but not as a torrent. It oozes through until it eventually makes a channel for itself. But, to begin with, it just oozes and brings with it a curious kind of knowing that there is somebody else there with you; you are not alone. That's a meditation you can do at any time, and it will work if you give it a chance. It won't happen in a crowded or noisy atmosphere; you have to obey the conditions. Nature is only conquered by obeying the law. You have to get your conditions just right with relaxation and rhythmic breathing. Sometimes a little incense or a lighted candle helps. Get yourself in the mood, get the right atmosphere about you, and stick to it day after day after day.

Question: In the zodiac, you have twelve signs which begin in Aries and end with Pisces. I've read that you live twelve lives and that you come in at Aries and go out at Pisces. I'm a Pisces!

W.E.B.: It's a very convenient method of manipulating the mind. You have to remember that the zodiac, as we know it, was rather different two thousand years ago. That zodiac at Dendera (Egypt) is different from the one we know today. But what is important is the way we think of the universe, the way we glyph it, the way we make symbols of ideas we have in connection with the universe. Leo, for instance, is a fiery sign, an outgoing person—the fighter and magnanimous warrior that gives the conquered a break. He/she is also the lion roaring when someone has taken its meat. You only have to look at a Leo to recognize one. These zodiacal signs are a very convenient classification, a coded information sheet that enables us to classify influences which we wouldn't otherwise be able to deal with. They allow you a concentrate of all those ideas into one symbol. The zodiac is simply a lot of pegs on which to hang certain group ideas which we have evolved. It's useful insofar as we keep it in perspective; but if you make a fetish of it, you're likely to be in trouble, get hung up about it. Remember the old adage, "The wise man rules his stars; only the fool obeys them." Because you come under the dominion of the planets and the stellar systems doesn't mean you lose all your will power; you don't become a puppet in their hands. These influences affect you, yes. They affect you in different ways, but you cannot be injured by them unless you allow yourself to be brainwashed into the belief, "It must be so because it's in my stars."

If Saturn is pressing heavily upon you, you can find a way to get out of the situation. You don't just lie down and let it do its damnedest. You adjust your conditions in order to lessen that Saturnian strain. You have to be like a sailor and steer against the wind by your own innate spiritual effort. Another little motto is, "The stars indicate; they do not compel." Tell an astrologer that and, if he's honest, he's bound to agree.

Chairman: I think what our friend there was getting at is the theory that you come in with Aries and go out with Pisces, and he's a little concerned he's not going to come back next time to sort out his problems.

W.E.B.: Oh, no, you can go round and round that zodiac time and time again. It's like being in a maze. You get to the middle and then you have to make your way out again. Some schools say you pass through every sign in order that you may get a full experience. I wouldn't like to comment on that. It may possibly be so for this reason: If it is necessary that we should be perfect as our Father in Heaven is perfect, we take on all experiences towards that end. We cannot be alien to anything. Like the Roman poet said, "I am a man and nothing in man's lot can be indifferent to me."[21] Therefore, if we are to reach that state of perfection, we must pass through all of those experiences in the planetary system.

You may possibly come back as Pisces again if you haven't learned the lesson that sign is trying to teach you in this life.

Question: Could you explain the theory of this phrase which has bothered me for a long time: "The sins of the fathers shall be visited upon the children?"[22] Does that mean our children inherit part of our karma?

W.E.B.: ". . . unto the third and fourth generation of them that hate me; And shewing mercy unto thousands of them that love me, and keep my commandments."[23] That's the whole passage, and it has to do with karma, certainly. Let me quote you another karmic passage: "For whatsoever a man soweth, that shall he also reap."[24] Say a man contracted syphilis which is passed on to his wife and thence to his child. That is karma for the wife and also for the child; and, at the same time, it is the result of the man's misdeed which is visited upon both the wife and child. But it's woe unto him who triggered it; the real result of that action comes back to the man himself. He can't dodge out of it; he must take on that karma and work it out. Still, both the child and the wife suffer. There is, however, another side to the story. The higher self of the child might take up that opportunity to work out a piece of karma from a previous life through the child's suffering; the wife may be reaping a seed of her own sowing, or, again, the higher self may take the opportunity to work off some past karma. But the man who started it all by transmitting the disease has to take on the karma for his actions, and this is made more difficult because he has triggered off karma for others. It comes round full circle to him like a boomerang; now he has to take on all that karma and more to put the balance right.

If that man accepts his karma philosophically and works it out, if he gains wisdom in the process and that wisdom is built into his consciousness as a permanent lesson, then he's won. In a similar way, if the higher self of the child sees that precipitated karma as an obstacle out of the way, a piece of karma worked out, then the child also gains. There could be a similar reaction for the wife. There's loss and gain all along the line. Karma is an intricate business. It needs a celestial computer to work it out and cannot be reduced to a few simple words such as "the sins of the fathers being visited upon the children." It works partly in that way, but the results can be very diverse because one person's misdeed can provide an opportunity for another to work out part of his or her karma. Contrariwise, it can add to the burden of another's karma, and the one who triggers that stores up a hefty chunk on his own account. These are examples of what you might call "good karma" and "bad karma."

There's one school of thought that says the "father" of that biblical phrase refers to reincarnation, that each personality is the father of the one that follows, and so on for each subsequent incarnation. It's not a philosophy I endorse myself, but I like to consider other people's beliefs and keep an open mind. But one thing is certain. We're all masters of ourselves; we are all creators of ourselves; we are all manipulators of ourselves. And sometimes we make an awful mess of it.

Question: Does the higher self influence you before you yourself can reach up to it?

W.E.B.: The higher self benevolently watches over you until you are capable of reaching up to it. When you are in a position to telephone it, then it replies. In the meantime, it watches and broods over you and doesn't let you drift too far off the path because it has a definite interest in your well–being. You are the tool it is going to use to conquer matter with, so it doesn't let you rust out in the rain. If it becomes necessary, it brings you in out of the storm. It's your guardian angel and has the subtle role of guarding you while at the same time not interfering. If you don't get the message from the higher self, you have to learn by experience, which is what happens more often than not. In a similar way, I might tell a child not to touch the stove because it is hot and will hurt him. If the child ignores the warning, he burns himself. We're all like that; we're told what we should do, what is right, and then we go off and do the opposite. But the higher self is very patient. It knows there is no death and so can afford to wait while we learn. But, as I said, it is always there brooding over you, trying to meet you half way.

And now—may the love and blessing of the Eternal be with you this night and always. Amen.

NOTES

W. E. BUTLER: A REMEMBRANCE

(1) Frederick W. H. Myers, *Saint Paul*, New Edition (New York: Macmillan & Co., 1885), p.6.

INTRODUCTION

(1) "I will not offer burned offerings unto the Lord my God that which doth cost me nothing." II Samuel 24:24.

(2) Mount Abiegnus, or *The Hill of Vision*, is the mystical mount of the Rosicrucians which is ascended in the higher consciousness. Its earthly symbol is Glastonbury Tor in Somerset, U.K. Under the mount is the cavern of the Rosy Cross where one may go in meditation. The cavern is vast and towering with a center altar. Above the altar is suspended the Rose Cross.

THE WESTERN TRADITION

(1) The Hermetic Order of the Golden Dawn (to give it its full title) was formed in 1887 and had a tremendous influence on occultism during the last part of the nineteenth century and well into the twentieth. It is still quoted today, in some quarters, as an authority on all things magical.

(2) The Society of the Inner Light was founded in 1922 by the late Dion Fortune. At her death she bequeathed her estate to the Society for the purpose of carrying on the work she began—the teaching of esoteric doctrines.

(3) James Russell Lowell (1819–1891) "The Present Crisis."

Lowell was professor of belles-lettres at Harvard in 1855.

(4) William Thomas Stead (1849–1912), journalist and editor of the Pall Mall Gazette; founded the *Review of Reviews* in 1890 and *Borderland,* a spiritualist magazine, in 1893; active and well-known in spiritualist circles; drowned in the *Titanic* disaster, 1912.

(5) Proverbs 24:3.

(6) Apocrypha I Esdras iv. 41.

TRAINING THE PERSONALITY: THE RUBBISH IN THE BACK ROOM

(1) An ideal state similar to Plato's *Republic* and Sir Thomas Moore's *Utopia*; described in a treatise, *La Città del Sole* (1623) by Dominican friar Tommaso Campanella (1568–1693).

(2) Erewhon, pronounced 'e-re-whon,' an ideal commonwealth in a slightly satirical novel of the same name by Samuel Butler; published anonymously in 1872; followed in 1901 with a sequel, *Erewhon Revisited*.

(3) A legendary island said to have existed in the Atlantic Ocean, first described by Plato in *Timaeus and Critias*; an ideal and prosperous state which came to be destroyed through the wickedness of its priests and statesmen. Much of the Mystery Teachings is said to have come originally from Atlantis. Many notable occultists and magicians, including Dion Fortune, believe in Atlantis and claim to have brought through teachings and memories of past lives in Atlantis. The Theosophist, W. Scott-Elliot, wrote a semi-scientific book complete with maps and entitled *The Story of Atlantis & Lost Lemuria,* published by Theosophical Publishing House in London. First published in 1896 and regularly revised and reprinted.

(4) *Confessions of St. Augustine* (of Hippo), Book i, sec 1. (Everyman Publication, London: Dent, and New York: Dutton), pp. 345–430.

(5) Alfred, Lord Tennyson, "The Passing of Arthur," line 407, *Idylls of the King*.

(6) Frederick Langbridge (1849–1923), *A Cluster of Quiet Thoughts* (Religious Tract Society Publication, 1986).

TRAINING THE PERSONALITY: THE GHOSTS IN THE PARLOR

(1) The evil and averse Sephiroth, their unbalanced and destructive essences.

(2) Nature spirits have been classified into the four kingdoms of the elements: the gnomes of the earth, the sylphs of air, the salamanders of fire, and the water spirits.

The gnomes of earth come under the rulership of the archangel Auriel; their king is Glob; and they are assigned to the North in a qabalistic temple.

The sylphs of the air are under the rulership of the archangel Raphael; their king is Paralda; and they are assigned to the East.

The salamanders of fire have their ruling archangel Michael; and their king is Djin; they are assigned to the South.

The water spirits (called undines) are under the rulership of the archangel Gabriel; their King is Necksa; and they are assigned to the West.

Many occultists and magicians believe the elementals come to aid them in their rites and invoke them accordingly.

(3) James 1:13–14.

(4) John Bunyan, *Pilgrim's Progress From this World to That Which is to Come*. First published in 1678, with many and varied editions following. An allegory in the form of a dream which sees the hero/pilgrim, Christian, fleeing from the City of Destruction through the "Slough of Despond" and other hazards. The Slough of Despond symbolizes the doubts and fears that beset mankind.

(5) Dion Fortune, *Moon Magic Being the Memoirs of a Mistress of that Art*, published posthumously in 1956 by Aquarian Press, London, with other editions following. *The Sea Priestess* was published by the author in 1938 and reissued by Aquarian Press (both vols still in print). *The Sea Priestess* and its sequel, *Moon Magic,* were both published in the U. S. in 1979 by Samuel Weiser, York Beach, Maine.

(6) I Corinthians 10:12.

(7) Ibid. 13:1–2.

(8) Henry Vaughan (1622–1695) *Silex Scintillans: Sacred Poems and Private Ejaculations,* 1650.

(9) Richard Bucke, *Cosmic Consciousness* (New York: E. P. Dutton, 1969).

(10) Luke 10:17.

(11) Acts of the Apostles 19:14–16.

(12) Frederick W. H. Myers, *Saint Paul,* Stanza 117, New Edition (New York: Macmillan & Co., 1885).

TRAINING THE PERSONALITY: THE ACTORS IN THE LOUNGE

(1) Alexander Pope (1688–1744) *An Essay on Man,* a series of philosophical poems, 1733–1734.

(2) I Kings 18:21–40.

(3) W. E. Butler, "The Magical Personality," *The Magician: His Training and Work* (Wellingborough, England: Aquarian Press, 1959).

(4) *The I Ching* or *Book of Changes,* an ancient Chinese method of divination. (See the Richard Wilhelm translation rendered into English by Cary F. Barnes, published by Routledge & Kegan Paul, London.)

(5) Paul Foster Case, *The Tarot: A Key to the Wisdom of the Ages.* (Richmond, Virginia: Macoy Publishing, 1947).

(6) Israel Regardie, *The Golden Dawn: An Account of the Teachings, Rites and Ceremonies of the Order of the Golden Dawn.* Originally in four vols, revised and enlarged in 1969 in two vols; several editions since. (Saint Paul, Minnesota: Llewellyn Publications).

(7) Ibid. Vol 2, page 280, chapter entitled "The Symbolism of the Seven Sides." Christian Rosenkreutz, legendary Lord of Light was founder of the Rosicrucian Movement. Whether R. C. actually lived or not is immaterial; it is what he stands for, the search for the Holy Grail, that really matters. For further information see *The Rosy Cross Unveiled* by Christopher McIntosh, Aquarian Press, 1980, and *The Chymical Wedding of Christian Rosenkreutz Anno 1459,* a modern introductory commentary on the same by Margaret Bennell and Isabel Wyatt, The Michael Press, Hawkwood College, Stroud, U.K.

(8) Mark 5:30.

(9) Dr. Friedrich Anton Mesmer (1733–1815) graduated as an M.D. in Vienna in 1766; founded and popularized the doctrine of mesmerism.

(10) James Braid (1795–1860), Scottish surgeon, graduated Edinburgh and practiced in Manchester; studied the phenomena of hypnotism extensively and coined the word *hypnotism*.

(11) Serious occultists and magicians keep a strict record of meditations, rites, and all magical work, which must be written up immediately after work is completed. This is known as the "Magical Diary" and is a very important part of the magician's equipment.

(12) William Shakespeare, *As You Like It*, Act 2, scene vii.

(13) Francis Bacon (1561–1626), *Apologie* iii, 152.

TRAINING THE PERSONALITY: THE FIRE DOWN BELOW

(1) Genesis I: 26–27.

(2) Zohar iii, 290a.

(3) Sir Henry Rider Haggard, *She*. First published in 1887 and reprinted in 1948 by Macdonald, London.

(4) The most up-to-date book by G. W. de la Warr, with Dr. Douglas Baker, is *Biomagnetism*, obtainable from the Radionics Association, Oxon, England.

(5) John Dee (1527–1608), mathematician, astrologer, and alchemist, in favor with Queen Elizabeth I as astrologer and adviser; later fell foul of James I. Some of his writings and the famous magic mirror are preserved in the British Museum. He teamed up with Edward Kelly (1555–1595), alchemist and apothecary, to study the occult sciences, including alchemy. Kelly was Dee's scryer in the spirit world. An account of Dr. Dee's magical works can be found in Richard Deacon's biographical study, *John Dee, Scientist, Geographer, Astrologer & Secret Agent to Elizabeth I* (London: Muller, 1968).

(6) An account of Nicholas Flamel's finding of the book entitled *Abraham the Jew* is preserved in *Nicholas Flamel, His Expositions of the Hieroglyphical Figures*, (London: Eiraneus Orandus), pp. 9–10. A long excerpt from the book is quoted by Manly P. Hall in

Masonic, Hermetic, Qabbalistic and Rosicrucian Symbolical Philosophy
(Los Angeles: The Philosophical Research Society), p. CLII.
(7) Romans 14:7.
(8) John Donne.
(9) Kim's Game: Ten to fifteen small items are placed on a tray
for the student to study. After an interval of two minutes the
items are covered or the tray removed. The student then makes
a list from memory of the articles, in the same order as they
appeared on the tray.
(10) Margaret Smith and Ian Jack, "Pippa Passes" (a drama),
part I, *The Poetical Works of Robert Browning* (Oxford English
Texts).

TRAINING THE PERSONALITY: ADONAI INTERNA

(1) C. G. Jung, *Flying Saucers: A Modern Myth* (London:
Routledge & Kegan Paul, 1958). Currently available from
Princeton University Press.
(2) "Paracelsus," part I, *The Poetical Works of Robert Browning*
(Oxford English Texts, 1982):
>   "Truth is within ourselves; it takes no rise
>   From outward things, whate'er you may believe: . ."
(3) Romans 8:38–39.

THE WITHDRAWN ORDER

(1) Alfred, Lord Tennyson, *In Memoriam,* xciv, verses 1 and 4.
(2) Hebrews 12:23.
(3) John 12:32.
(4) Ibid. 3:14.
(5) Samuel Rogers (1763–1855) *Human Life,* 1.49 (1819). At the
time of Wordsworth's death, in 1850, Rogers was offered the
Poet Laureateship but declined the honor.
(6) Dante Alighieri, "Paradise," Canto XXXIII, lines 134 and
135, *The Vision of Dante* or *Hell, Purgatory, and Paradise,* translated
by the Rev. Henry F. Cary in 1982.
(7) Ibid., Canto III, line 85.

WOVEN PACES AND WAVING HANDS

(1) Alfred Lord Tennyson, *Idylls of the King*, Merlin and Vivien (last part).

(2) Dion Fortune, *The Secrets of Dr. Taverner*, (Saint Paul: Llewellyn Publications, 1962). First published in 1926. "The Power House" is the eleventh and last story in the book—fiction woven around fact. The nursing home which is the backdrop for the short stories did actually exist. Dr. Taverner in real life was Dr. Moriarty, Dion Fortune's teacher.

(3) Lewis Carroll, *The Hunting of the Snark* (1876), first fitment: verse 2.

(4) Rudyard Kipling (1865–1936), *In the Neolithic Age,* last verse, last line.

(5) S. L. MacGregor Mathers, *The Sacred Magic of Abramelin the Mage*. Published in 1898. Translated from the French from an old document Mathers found in the Bibliothèque d'Arsènal in Paris.

(6) *Theurgy* from the Greek meaning "divine work" is a system of magic to invoke divine or other beneficial gods and spirits to aid magical rites.

(7) Iamblichus, *Theurgia* or *The Egyptian Mysteries*. Reply of Abammon, the Teacher, to *The Letter of Porphyry to Anebo;* together with "Solutions of the Questions Therein Contained." Translated from the Greek by Alexander Wilder, M.D., FAS. (London: Rider, 1911).

(8) David Edwards, *Dare to Make Magic* (London: Rigel Press, 1971).

QUESTIONS AND ANSWERS

(1) Luke 17:21.

(2) Dr. Douglas Baker, *Esoteric Psychology: The Seven Rays*, vol 5, part one of *The Seven Pillars of Ancient Wisdom*. Published in 1975 by the author under the imprint, "Little Elephant," Essendon, Herts, England.

(3) Roland Hunt, *The Seven Keys to Colour Healing* (Essex, En-

gland: The C. W. Daniel Company, 1971). Also *The Eighth Key to Colour* and *Self-Analysis and Clarification Through Colour.* (London: Fowler, 1965).

(4) Theo Gimbel, *Healing Through Colour* and *Colour, Form, Sound and Healing.* Both vols published by the C. W. Daniel Co., Essex, London.

(5) William G. Gray, *Ladder of Lights,* or *Qabalah Renovata* (Cheltenham: Helios Book Services, 1968).

(6) Israel Regardie, *Tree of Life: A Study in Magic.* (York Beach, Maine: Samuel Weiser, 1983).

(7) Dion Fortune, *Mystical Qabalah* (York Beach, Maine: Samuel Weiser, 1984). First published in 1935 by Ernest Benn, London.

(8) S. L. MacGregor Mathers, *The Kabbalah Unveiled,* containing the following Books of the Zohar: *The Book of Concealed Mystery, The Greater Holy Assembly, The Lesser Holy Assembly* (York Beach, Maine: Samuel Weiser, 1983). First published in 1887.

(9) Johann Wolfgang von Goethe, *Theory of Colours,* translated from the German with notes by Charles Lock Eastlake. Published in 1840 by John Murray, London. Modern editions available from The M.I.T. Press, Cambridge, Massachusetts, and London, England.

(10) Eleanor C. Merry & Maria Schindler, *Pure Colour.* Part One, *Goethe's Theory of Colour Applied*; Part Two, *Painting and Imagination*; Part Three, *Extracts from Goethe's Scientific Work.* Published in London in 1946. Currently out of print.

(11) Hildegard the Venerable, *To Isis Sophia* (eleventh century).

(12) *The Song of the Lord Bhagavadgita* (II Sankhya, pp. 34–35), translated by Edward J. Thomas in 1931. Reprinted in 1959 by John Murray, London, Wisdom of the East series.

(13) Anna (Bonus) Kingsford & Edward Maitland, "Exhortation of Hermes to his Neophyte," *Addresses and Essays on Vegetarianism* (London: Watkins, 1912), p. 211.

(14) Ibid.

(15) Sir Edwin Arnold (1832–1904) *The Light of Asia* or *The Great Renunciation.*

(16) Ibid.

(17) Ibid.

(18) Charles Fort, *The Book of the Damned* and *New Lands*. (New York: Grosset & Dunlap). Also, *The Complete Books of Charles Fort* (New York: Dover Publications, 1975).

(19) Adapted from:

> Lead me from the unreal to the real;
> Lead me from darkness to light;
> Lead me from death to immortality.

From the *Bridhadaranyaka-Upanishad*

(20) Revelations 1:18.

(21) Terence (190–159 B.C.), *Heauton Timoroumenos* I:77.

(22) Exodus 20:5–6.

(23) Ibid.

(24) Galatians 6:7.

INDEX